MISSIONS FROM THE MODERN VIEW

MISSIONS FROM THE MODERN VIEW

ROBERT A. HUME

GYAN

Published by

Gyan Publishing House
5, Ansari Road
Daryaganj, New Delhi-110002
Phone: 011-47034999, 9811692060
E-mail: books@gyanbooks.com

Distribution Network
gyanbooks.com
India, USA, Canada, UK, Australia

ISBN: 978-93-7133-602-4 (PB)

First Published, 1905

2nd Impression 2025

Printed at: Gyan Press, Delhi.

MISSIONS FROM THE MODERN VIEW
Author: ROBERT A. HUME

MISSIONS FROM THE MODERN VIEW

MISSIONS FROM THE MODERN VIEW

BY

ROBERT A. HUME

OF

AHMEDNAGAR, INDIA

WITH AN INTRODUCTION BY

CHARLES CUTHBERT HALL

TO MY WIFE

INTRODUCTION

THE lectures following contribute to the solution of a problem at once intricate and fascinating. That problem is the readjustment of missionary ideals and methods to the modern state of knowledge. To admit the need of readjustment in the field of missions is to place that field in the same honorable category with every other field of lofty human enterprise. Readjustment means growth, progress, augmentation of power, as the effects of increased knowledge and experience. It would be mistaken loyalty to great leaders of the past to contend that their successors in work must occupy the same point of view and practice the same methods. The great leaders of the past, could they speak to us, would protest against such well-meant but erroneous conservatism. They themselves were prophets, gazing beyond the things they saw, and testifying beforetime of a better day to come after them. William Carey, of Serampore, was a statesman and a prophet. None can stand in his library, or look upon his buildings on the river bank, or trace the outline of his missionary policy without realizing that his mind anticipated and foresaw developments of opinion and method that must in time reconstruct the thinking of Christian missionaries in many particulars. The prophecies of some of these early leaders are being fulfilled. The literatures and religions of the East are studied in the West. The strategic posts of service in India and the Far East are occupied by an increasing number of men whose training, historically, philosophically, socially, qualifies them to see clearly and to handle tactfully the most splendid problem of modern times, the Christianization of the Asiatic consciousness.

It is correct and necessary that in the readjustment of missionary ideals and methods the initiative shall be taken by missionaries themselves and not by their academic advisers and critics at home. Without doubt there are aspects of the situation that can best be realized at long range, by those who are not involved in the responsibilities and limitations of denominational service abroad. Many missionaries are disqualified, by unavoidable conditions, for a judgment of authority upon the true policy of the Church in erecting Christian institutions in non-Christian lands. Stationed in remote communities; absorbed in local operations; restricted, perhaps, by the sectarian spirit of the ecclesiastical body to which they are responsible; deprived of opportunities for travel and extensive generalization, not a few members of the foreign missionary force are relatively unacquainted with contemporary Eastern opinion, in circles of influence. As compared with the limited field of missionaries thus situated, it is probable that an intelligent and sympathetic view is more readily attained at a distance and under conditions absolved from sectarian restraint. But the view thus obtained is likely to be invalidated, in important particulars, by lack of local knowledge. The armchair theorists of the West may endeavor to be fair, and may actually possess a substantial basis of technical information. But without first-hand knowledge of the Eastern land, the Eastern atmosphere, the Eastern mind and soul, all theory formulated in the West may be fallacious. Hence the necessity that, in the readjustment of missionary ideals and methods, the initiative shall proceed from those whose experience in the field is co-ordinated with broad theoretical training. It is one of many splendid features of modern missionary activity that persons are to be found at important posts of foreign duty who join ripe experience with thoroughgoing culture. These are they to whom all parties in interest must look, for correct interpretations of existing conditions and fertile suggestions of procedure. It is very striking to observe that these modern leaders, although allied ecclesiastically with Churches of the West that perpetuate hereditary divergences of doctrine and practice, are agreed in certain fundamental positions. They are quite at one in recognizing that the heart of the East already contains the principle of religious aspiration, and is hungering and thirsting for God. They agree that the policy of Christian Missions toward existing religious experience must be that of Christ, Who came not to destroy but to fulfill; to conserve the reality, however dwarfed or perverted in mode of expression, and to invest that deficient reality with the rich content of the revelation of God in Christ Jesus. They agree that the Christianization of the Asiatic consciousness does not mean its transformation into the likeness of the West; and that the Mission of the Holy Ghost in the East may be to produce an Oriental Christianity different in institutional form and in temperament from the Christianity of Europe and America.

Dr. Hume's lectures admirably illustrate the readjustment of ideals and methods that has taken place already in the most intelligent circles of foreign missionary workers. These lectures are a gospel for the West. They show

how far beyond much of our relatively narrow and provincial thinking many of our foremost missionaries have advanced. They summon the Church at home to rise to a higher plane of thought; to abandon the discussion of out-worn points of controversy; to awake from the sleep of luxury, formalism, and self-centered religious profession; to respect the aspirations and interests of Eastern peoples; to advance to an adequate maintenance of scholarly and consecrated men who, by lives of purity and excellence, have disarmed the suspicions and won the respect of Orientals. These great missionary leaders know the situation as it exists. They know how to reach, and they are reaching, the religious consciousness of Asia. They know how to conduct wise operations for the propagation of Christianity in lands for which the Son of God gave His very life. Those operations, conceived in wisdom, conducted in love, are crippled in the most piteous manner by lack of money to maintain them. The Christian churches of the West include in their membership the possessors of enormous wealth. To them may this book speak in tones that shall instruct the intellect, admonish the conscience, and enlarge the heart.

Charles Cuthbert Hall.

Union Theological Seminary, *June, 1905.*

AUTHOR'S NOTE

The first six chapters of this book consist of lectures which were delivered at Andover Theological Seminary, the University of Chicago, the Chicago Theological Seminary, and Bangor Theological Seminary. The last two chapters are exact illustrations of how I have given the Christian message to Indians.

R. A. Hume.

Springfield, Mass., May, 1905.

CONTENTS

I

MISSIONS FROM THE MODERN VIEW OF GOD AND THE WORLD

THE modern view of God and the world is profoundly affecting every other sphere of thought and duty except missions. But the world is one; its solidarity is more and more recognized. Thought and life in one department affect thought and life in other departments. In part, the modern view is a result of foreign missions. Therefore, of course this modern view must affect thought about missions and work by missionaries. In fact, foreign missions ought to be, and truly are, the expression by Christian people of their understanding of their relations to God and the world, under the inspiration of the Lord Jesus Christ and according to His principles. The modern view of God and the world is larger and more vital than the old one. It brings God most near to every single member of the world. The nearer view of almost everything gives a fuller and truer view. Every modern poet and every modern commanding thinker who believes in God at all emphasizes the evidence of God in His world and His ceaseless activity, not only in every part of the physical world, but also in every part of the moral world of men.

> "Speak to Him, thou, for He heareth,
> And spirit with spirit may meet;
> Closer is He than breathing
> And nearer than hands or feet."

This throbbing, vital recognition of God as ceaselessly active in every man is the idea of theistic evolution which is the formative principle of modern thought. Law is no longer thought of as an impersonal force, but as an expression of personal will. Just as laws of physical nature, so laws of human nature, are considered the expression of God's customary action. Theistic evolution leaves no essential distinction between the natural and the supernatural. They are both alike divine. Therefore there is no essential difference between revealed and natural religion. God is light and therefore ever revealing Himself. Men are made in God's image and are fitted to know Him. But because men are weak and erring, they very partially understand God. The religion of any company of men is their interpretation in thought and in practice of what God is trying to teach them. Because of their limitations and their sins, they only partially, and often very imperfectly, understand what He is trying to teach. But there is no proper distinction between true and false religions. A more proper term would be less perfect and more perfect religions. Every religion has something of truth in it, because it recognizes the existence of God, the fact of His relation to men, and of His activity toward them, and the importance of men's relations to God being made right. Yet every religion is still imperfect. According to the definition of religion just given, even the Christian religion has not yet attained to full-orbed apprehension of all spiritual things in their right proportions. This is exactly the teaching of Jesus Christ, who said to His disciples, "I have yet many things to say unto you, but ye cannot bear them now. Howbeit when He, the Spirit of truth is come, He shall guide you into all the truth." The apostle Paul wrote in one of his letters, "I fed you with milk, not with meat; for ye were not able to bear it; nay, not even now are ye able." This is but another way of saying that Christianity is a growing religion. The fundamental and sufficient evidence that Islam cannot be the religion of thinking men in modern times is the fact that it claims to be, and is, a religion full-grown, as it is laid down in the Quran. Islam knows no doctrine of theistic evolution. If Christianity were a religion full-grown and limited to such interpretation of its principles as was known even by the inspired writers of the Bible, it would not be a growing religion, suited to the universal needs of all men of all times. Just because it is a growing religion, it has the possibilities of being universal in its power to meet the religious needs of mankind. Hence, the fullest interpretation of spiritual needs at any time, though it be the fullest up to that time, must of necessity be partial. But this is no more discreditable to religion than the same principle is to science. It is because science is growing knowledge that it is able to modify the life of every generation.

Science is nothing else than one witness to God's infinite greatness and readiness to reveal Himself and to communicate Himself to his children just as fast and as far as by seeking and following His laws they have developed capacity and willingness to understand Him. As science is simply God's revelation of Himself in one sphere to patient and obedient men who seek to know and do His will in one direction, so in another sphere religion is the witness of His infinite greatness and readiness to reveal Himself and to communicate Himself to His children just as fast and as far as they develop capacity and willingness to hear Him and take His help in spiritual things. The apostle Paul never uttered a more inspired word than when he said, "I know only in part, and I teach only in part; but more and more the perfect is going to come, and as perfection gradually comes, that which is partial will be done away. Now I know only in part, but then shall I know fully." For substance that is only saying that Paul's religion was a growing religion. One of the most interesting features in the study of his letters is to notice how he grew in his interpretation of spiritual things.

The modern view also emphasizes the fact that salvation is not essentially a matter of time and place, but is a matter of character. Salvation is spiritual soundness. It is an ethical condition. But this is exactly what the Lord Jesus Christ most plainly taught. He said very little about what would happen to men when they had gone to heaven. He said that He came that men might have life and that they might have it abundantly, and that men who take His help would have eternal life *now*. "He that hath the Son hath eternal life."

A great deal of modern Christian thought, while not denying the metaphysical divinity of Christ, dwells principally upon His ethical divinity, which is just what would naturally follow when the salvation which He came to give to men was ethical soundness of character. Jesus Christ is the human expression of God. God is like Jesus Christ. From this follows the further consideration which Jesus Christ most plainly and most helpfully taught: that God is in a true sense like men. When the Lord Jesus Christ wanted to help men to understand how simple, how real, how vital is God's relation to every man, and how anxious God is to have every human child of His come to Him in simplicity with every thought and need, He said for substance, This is the way to think of God in relation to you. You may be sure that He will do to you even better than you would do to your own son. If your son were hungry and asked you for bread, would you not give him bread? And if he asked you also for fish, would you not give him a fish? You would not give him a serpent, would you? Well, if you, with your limitations and your sins, if you, being evil, do as well as you can by your own children, how much more shall your Heavenly Father do the best that He can by every one of His human children; and the best that He can do is to give His Holy Spirit to make you holy.

Modern Christian thought is rightly making the Holy Spirit truly universal in His presence and activity. Christian thought has always emphasized the divinity of the Holy Spirit, but it failed to recognize His omnipresence and His universal activity. In no respect does the modern doctrine of the immanence of God so largely and so helpfully enrich modern thought and life as in recognition of the omnipresent activity of the Holy Spirit. If the Holy Spirit is truly God, then He is God in the heart of every man trying to make him holy.

Modern Christian thought rightly emphasizes historicity as very important in the consideration of all religious matters, for exact history is a statement and interpretation of facts with which God has been connected as well as with which man has been connected. It is one of the principal excellences of the Christian religion that it seeks to know the exact facts of history, whether those facts are according to the traditional explanation or different from that explanation. History is and ever will be one door and way to the life of God. But modern Christian thought is coming more and more to recognize that even historicity is not the complete or the chief evidence in spiritual things. History is only the story of the past. It cannot give the ideal of the future. But the ideal is an important part of religion, both as a system of thought and as a life, because it is the future that draws spirits onward and upward more than the past that drives them on. The lowest grades of life have an outlook simply upon the past and recognize only the possibility and compulsion of the past. One fundamental weakness in the doctrine of transmigration and of reincarnation, which are the principal forces in Hinduism, is that it is wholly, or mainly, the past that controls the future. But poets and seers and all lovers know that the present and the future are more than the past. Therefore, while not ignoring the past or the present, they care for the past principally because it is the door into a greater future. That is, the lure of the ideal is the formative influence in the life of the poet and the seer and the lover. It is the hope of greater and better things that makes men climb mountains and cross oceans and suffer difficulties with patience and with delight, because there is more light and life and joy in the ideal which is luring them on. It is the ideal which makes the patriot, the teacher, the parent, the lover.

Proportion is more and more coming to be seen to be the important thing in religion, as in every other sphere of life. Good cooking is largely a matter of proportion. Too much or too little of an ingredient, over-baking or under-baking, injures any meal. In the matter of amusements sanity and proper results depend mainly upon the proportion of time, strength, and money given to any one amusement, or to amusements as a part of strenuous life. Proportion is the principal thing in any wise use of money. Modern life makes the study and practice of proportion almost its chief business. The same thing applies in religion. Every religion and every denomination in the Christian religion has its weakness in over-emphasizing some phase of truth and under-emphasizing others. But Jesus Christ is the explanation of the riddle of religion, as of all life. He gave all religious principles in right proportion. He grew just as we grow. But He was God manifest in the flesh in the fullest measure possible for God to reveal Himself through men. Yet even He said, "I tell you the truth. It is expedient for you that I go away, for if I go not away, the Comforter will not come unto you; but if I go, I will send Him unto you. When He, the Spirit of truth is come, He shall guide you into all truth." The marvel is that no one has ever gone beyond the Lord Jesus Christ. No one has appeared who has the slightest possibility of going beyond Him. And most, if not all, of the great spiritual seers say that they get their inspiration and their light largely from Jesus Christ. They reverently acknowledge their dependence upon Him and their obligation to Him. Even now He is rising still higher and higher in the spiritual firmament of the whole world. He is still the Light of the World.

The modern view of God is largely the modern view of the world. The world is larger because God is larger. It is not now only or mainly physical nature which is thought of as revealing God. Men are considered as His chief revelation. This is simply in accordance with the teachings of Christ and true Christianity. It is the natural inference from the whole doctrine of incarnation. God was manifest in supremest human form in Jesus Christ in order that He might manifest Himself also in every other man. Probably the finest word in the Apocalypse is this: "And I heard a great voice out of the throne saying, Behold, the tabernacle of God is with men, and He shall dwell with them and they shall be his people, and God himself shall be with them, and be their God; and He shall wipe away every tear from their eyes." Therefore, in stating the modern view of God I have already stated the modern view of God and the world. God is in His world. Men are made in His image. They are His children. He is ever trying to do His very, very best by every one of them. They are very imperfect. They very partially and imperfectly understand Him. They very often fail to take His help. In this way they sin against Him and fail to do their duty. They grieve Him, but He is so patient, so patient.

> "Take all in a word, the trust in God's breast
> Lies trace for trace, on ours impressed.
> Though He is so bright and we are so dim,
> We are made in His image, we witness Him."

Now how does this modern view of God and of the world affect missions? Of course, the main thought and impulse of Christian missions is the desire to help in bringing the world of men into that conscious relation to their Father God, which He desires, and which Christ came to secure. With the view-point of God and the world here expressed missions would naturally be the very first sphere of thought and activity to be changed. So the modern view does two things for missions.

First: It brings into nobler light the Christ-likeness which has characterized foreign missions from apostolic times to the present, in the actual going out of Christian men and women at self-sacrifice and with enthusiastic love to make known to brother-men and sister-women that knowledge and love of God which Jesus Christ had revealed to the missionaries themselves. It was a narrower view of God and of the world than the modern view which inspired those missionaries, but it is the more honorable to those heroic men and women that they went with the motive which they had; that they proved the sincerity and intensity of their sense of brotherhood and fellowship and their filial relation to their Heavenly Father by going and loving and suffering as they did. It ill becomes the critics of those men and women, who plume themselves on their larger thought, to criticise those who, from a narrower view, went as missionaries of the

Cross; whereas all that many of those critics have done for their fellowmen has been to sit at ease at home and to throw stones at the men who proved their sense of brotherhood by going to the front and helping men as they could.

Secondly: This modern view vastly increases the hopefulness and the importance of missions. Since God is at work on every man; since most men, with their limitations and their sins, fail to apprehend God as He wishes them to apprehend Him; since the Lord Jesus Christ is the fullest revelation of God; and since the Holy Spirit uses the Lord Jesus Christ and His revelation of spiritual truth as His best instrument in bringing men into conscious filial relations with their Heavenly Father, how inspiring the opportunity and how imperative the duty of taking to those who do not know Christ the inspiration and the power which He longs to give them! The larger and nearer view of God brings encouragement to every child of His who tries to bring this larger view into the horizon of every other man. The universality of religion which is now recognized is a new illustration of God's activity in every man. The universality of the Holy

Spirit's work is a call to give to the Holy Spirit that instrument which He especially needs in enabling God to make men come into fuller and fuller light, and thus to grow in holiness. The Lord Jesus Christ truly said, "When the Comforter is come, He will convict the world in respect of sin, and of righteousness, and of judgment: of sin because they believe not on me." "He shall take of mine, and shall declare it unto you."

A new confidence and joy in God's eternal love is always awakened in every land by that revelation of God's own yearning for the love of His weak and erring human children which was made by the life and sacrifice of His well-beloved Son Jesus Christ. The Christian missionary now goes to the non-Christian world under the inspiration of the thought that not only are *men* missing the love and confidence and intelligent fellowship with their Father which they need, but that the Heavenly Father himself craves, with infinite longing and love, the intelligent fellowship and love and confidence of each child of His. So that God is suffering for lack of returning love from His children, just as human parents suffer from the sins of their heedless and willful children perhaps more than those heedless and willful children suffer from their neglect of parental love. It was this thought of the suffering of God on account of His children being unreconciled to Him that led the apostle to the Gentiles to say, "We are ambassadors on behalf of Christ, as though God were entreating by us; we beseech you on behalf of Christ, be ye reconciled to God."

This modern view and more spiritual interpretation of the work of Christ also gives a new glory and urgency to foreign missions from the thought that just as Jesus Christ came to "fulfill" the partial view of the Judaic system, so also He came to "fulfill" the partial interpretation of God which men in other religions have made. To "fulfill" means to "fill full." That is what Jesus Christ did to the Judaic system. With spiritual principle He filled full the partial and limited views of the earlier prophets of Israel. The Jews of His time did not adequately understand Him. But herein is the unique character of the Lord Jesus Christ. Herein is He shown to be the Saviour of the world that by His teachings and life and sacrifice and death and resurrection He gave such a revelation of God as even now men have only partially understood. And He not only gave the revelation, but He gives power to live according to that revelation. The modern view shows that God has always been at work on other peoples besides the ancient children of Israel; and that just as "in the fullness of time" Jesus Christ came to fulfill the limited interpretations of the Judaic system, so Christ is the fulfiller of earlier and more partial teachings of God which have been current in His human children in any land and at any time. That phrase, "fullness of time," is one of the finest in the literature of mankind, and one of the most illuminating words of the apostle Paul. It is a thought essential to modern theistic evolution. It expresses something like the modern phrase, "the psychological moment." Jesus Christ is the fulfillment and the fulfiller of all spiritual truth. What a new inspiration to foreign missions, that, since the light of the glorious gospel of the blessed God has been committed to our trust, we should let it shine through us upon all the world; that those who have not seen this light, might see and walk and rejoice in it, as many of those who live in Christian lands now do. It is an inspiration to foreign missions that through our holding forth Christ to those who do not know Him He may see of the travail of His soul and be satisfied. For He said, "Other sheep I have which are not of this fold: them also I must bring and they shall hear my voice; and they shall become one flock, one shepherd."

This modern view of God and the world affects the assumptions of the missionary in other ways. It emphasizes the fact that some of the weaknesses of the non-Christian world which have been thought to be sinful, are rather more phases of ignorance than sin, and it makes some phases of sin more prominent and heinous than they have been previously thought to be. For example: Whereas the older view made idolatry one of the worst sins of non-Christians, the new view makes idolatry more ignorance than sin. It is not because the idolater knows that idols are not the proper symbol of God, and, knowing this, still makes and worships them, but because he is feeling after God, and having no such spiritual revelation of Him as the Christian has in the Lord Jesus Christ, through idols he ignorantly gropes after the real God whom he can approach. But this modern view is really the Christian view. It is the view which the apostle Paul preached when he said on Mars Hill to the Athenians, who were using idols, "What ye worship in *ignorance*, this I set forth unto you." Similarly, caste in India is now seen to have grown out of social institutions such as the color line, trade guilds, differences in education, property, and locality, in a way not intentionally wrongful or unkind, though the final result of that system has been to develop some of the most unlovely and unbrotherly characteristics in the relations of men, and though it would be an awful sin if persisted in under the light of the Christian Gospel. But, on the contrary, this modern view of God and the world emphasizes in a new and unexpected light the sin and the selfishness of the dweller in Christian lands who has had the fuller revelation of God which comes through Jesus Christ and the countless privileges of Christian civilization, in not caring for his non-Christian brother enough to give him the same life and help, even at the cost of self-sacrifice. It has given a new illustration of the parable of the Good Samaritan. No intelligent visitor to non-Christian lands like India and Burma and China and Africa and the islands of the seas, but knows that polytheism, pantheism, idolatry, caste, ignorance, child-marriage, poverty, and other ills from which millions upon millions in those lands are suffering are like blows from which the man fell bleeding on the way from Jerusalem to Jericho. So those who, dwelling in Christian lands, smugly comfort themselves on their superior enlightenment and sneer at the missionary as narrow and fanatical, are truly like the Levite and the priest who passed by on the other side, while the missionary is the good Samaritan who goes to the bleeding man, and binds up his wounds, and puts him on his own beast, and takes him to an inn, and provides for him. The truth that men in non-Christian lands, as much as those in Christian lands, really need the revelation of God which comes through Christ and the inspiration and power which He gives, is shown by the restlessness of non-Christian peoples, by their vague, mistaken efforts to relieve themselves from spiritual burdens through austerities and pilgrimages and gifts to idols. Captain Cornelius was indeed "a devout man and one that feared God with all his house, who gave much alms to the poor and prayed to God always." But with all his devoutness he was not satisfied, and when the apostle Peter told him about the Lord Jesus Christ and frankly admitted that he himself was now finding out more and more than he had previously understood, since "God is no respecter of persons: but in every nation he that feareth Him and worketh righteousness is acceptable to Him," that devout non-Christian, instead of saying, "Very well, if that is so, then I do not see any need of my becoming a Christian," said just the opposite. He said, That is just the revelation of God which I have been longing for and need, and I wish this very hour with all my household, to enroll myself as His humble disciple; and he and his family were then baptized and entered the Christian fold. So now this larger view of God as trying to reveal Himself to every man, and of his Spirit's universal activity in the hearts of men, instead of leading non-Christians who hear this call to think that they do not need the Lord Jesus Christ, would naturally have and does have the opposite effect when the Christian evangel is preached to them in this large way.

With this view of God and the world, in loyalty to the Lord Jesus Christ and under His inspiration, the aims of the modern missionary are not really very unlike what the aims of the missionary were under a more contracted view. Yet the way of conceiving and stating those aims is different. A statement of those aims might be put in modern language somewhat like this: First, the Christian missionary now aims to create a new Christian climate, somewhat as the Lord Jesus Christ sought to create it; as the apostle Paul and the apostle Peter sought to create it; *i. e.*, so to shed abroad the light of the gospel that men in non-Christian lands shall make the same assumptions which men in Christian lands now make. Those assumptions are something like these: That there is only one God, who is the Father of the spirits as well as of the bodies of all men; that He is ever present with every human child and trying to do His best for the spirit of every child; that because God is thus the Father of us all, we are all brothers and sisters of one another; that, therefore, we should realize the mutual interest of each human being in every other human being; and that it is both the privilege and the duty of every man to do his best, as for the body, so for the spirit of every fellowman. And the aim is that men, growing up in these assumptions, shall live as sons of God. With these assumptions and trying to live according to them, whether men join the Christian church or not, they *are* in the kingdom of God; and just so far as the Church becomes co-terminous with the kingdom of God, they will sooner or later become members of the Christian Church.

Second: the missionary aims to make better men and women, and so to make a better world. He does not talk much about men's going to a safe place called heaven because Jesus Christ died, whether men take His help and become saved into good character in this world or not. Over the door of the room in which I meet men who come to talk with me I have placed, in spirit, though not in words, the sign, "R. A. Hume, maker and mender of men and boys on the Jesus Christ pattern by the help of the Lord Jesus Christ." If helping non-Christians to become Christians does not make better men and women, better husbands and wives, better fathers and mothers, better children, better neighbors, better citizens, and better friends, then the missionary of the modern view would not have accomplished what he aims to accomplish. It is because under the older and more contracted view there had been some who professed the name of Christian, but who did not become better men and women, yet who in ignorance or sin made the Christian profession, and thus were a dishonor to the Lord Jesus whose name they took, and to the missionary who meant to do them good, that travelers and others have, in some places, with some degree of reason, thought missions were doing no good and were even doing harm. But in very truth among men in every land about which I am informed the majority of those who have come into the vision of the Lord Jesus and who have confessed themselves His disciples, have through His help become better men and women, with a larger and fuller life.

Third: The missionary aims to ascertain so far as he can, and to thank God for, every truth which He has taught to any man in any form and in any degree. Then with thoughtful recognition of this work of God the missionary seeks to adapt from the Christian interpretation of things that which will supplement and fulfill and bring into rightness the truth which God has in part revealed to the non-Christian. In other words, under the modern view of God and the world the modern missionary believes that, in the fullness of time, God through Jesus Christ is fulfilling that which He had previously taught any men in part.

Fourth: The modern missionary realizes that since Jesus Christ has come that all men might have life and might have it more abundantly, it is his privilege and duty to help them in everything that would enrich their life. In this the modern missionary is practically doing simply what all missionaries have more or less done from the first. With a different view of God and the world they wrought better than they knew. From the first the missionary in India has been a pioneer in all that enriches life. He was a pioneer in higher English education; in primary education among the ignorant masses; in education for women, and in all that upbuilds and ennobles women; in medical work of all kinds; and now by common consent the missionary is the pioneer in the most successful and useful lines of industrial training and development.

Missionaries like Livingston and Cyrus Hamlin may or may not have had any idea of theistic evolution, but at heart they had the modern view of God and the world, and they did the kind of work which is bringing about that modern view. It now gives justification to a matter which was long a source of doubt and debate, and which in some missionary circles brought even condemnation to certain lines of missionary activity. In the narrow conception that all that the missionary ought to do is to tell men that Christ died for their sins and that if they believed in Him He would forgive them and take them to heaven, there was no adequate justification for the missionary's spending strength and time in educating people in schools, in carrying on medical work except to a very limited extent, and certainly no justification for efforts to improve the social and economic condition of peoples in other lands. Nevertheless, most missionaries have always felt moved to do something in these directions, and this has led to frequent and often acrimonious discussions in some circles as to whether the efforts of medical missionaries were quite legitimate. But what the logic of the heart and of the situation led most missionaries to do, even despite the then prevailing theory of missions, can now find joyous acceptance, because these more philanthropic efforts are seen to be entirely consistent with the true spirit of Christ. Therefore, now some people in the spirit of Jesus are well pleased to give money and effort for medical and industrial missons, even when through narrow and mistaken conceptions they are unwilling to do anything for the more fundamental and more important work of giving to non-Christians that knowledge of God the Father of our spirits, and of the consequent brotherhood of men, which are unquestionably the chief things in the Christian religion and the most important benefits which this religion imparts to mankind.

Hence, this modern view is making missionary work not so much ecclesiastical as personal, and is making the betterment of the social and economic conditions of brother-men and sister-women in non-Christian lands the duty and the privilege of their more favored fellowmen in Christendom. In other words, the largest and most promising missionary activity is now considered to be the all round work of spiritual, mental, and physical betterment, because such three-fold comprehensive endeavor best brings men into that abundance of life which God through Jesus Christ desires to give them.

This outlook will also give to laymen more and more part in the various lines of missionary activity. In Christian lands at home laymen are finding larger and larger spheres of influence. Similarly, laymen are to do a much larger part in foreign missionary work. The larger scope of such work demands that kind of qualification which often laymen possess more than the average clergyman. And as foreign laymen set the example in the manifold developments of missionary efforts, so they will stimulate indigenous Christian laymen in other lands to see how large a sphere is open for them in making their own lands Christian.

This view affects missions helpfully not only by holding up new motives for inspiration and added hope to missionary zeal, but it will also improve missionary methods as well. It will make insight into the characteristics of non-Christian peoples and institutions more necessary and helpful. And since insight and sympathy are sisters, the new view will also increase sympathy in the selection and exercise of missionary methods. It will make the study and adaptation of methods and motives more important. It will use the adjective "better" for commending the Christian religion to non-Christians rather than the adjective "best." But this is simply in accordance with Biblical ideas and precedents. The characteristic word in the Epistle to the Hebrews is the adjective "better." "We have a better High Priest, a better hope, a better testament, a better covenant, a better sacrifice, a better substance, a better country, better things," etc. "God having provided some better thing concerning us, that apart from us they should not be made perfect." As in the first century so now, the adjective "better" is the right expression for the earlier relation of Christianity to the ethnic faiths. It is the word which expresses the gradual fulfillment of vague and undeveloped aspirations. Since it is always most difficult to establish a universal proposition, one should not attempt more than is necessary in any undertaking. Moreover, since Christianity is a growing religion, and since some phases of thought and life which have seemed to Christians at one time to be absolutely the best, have, after added knowledge and experience, been seen to be not full-orbed apprehension of spiritual truth, the adjective "better" is the only correct term and conception to be used by the Christian teacher in any department of thought and life. Moreover, from my own missionary experience I can assure you that whereas a statement by a Christian missionary that the Christian religion is absolutely the best religion in the world, strikes the cultivated non-Christian as offensive and as claiming too much, presenting that same religion as better than those which have been followed by non-Christians hitherto receives a more ready and respectful acceptance than any other way of teaching the helpfulness of the Lord Jesus Christ.

This modern view of missions, based on a new view of God and the world, seems to some people to do away with the need, or at least with the urgency, of foreign missionary effort at all. They sometimes say, "If God is now trying to do all He can for every man in the world, and if His Spirit's activity is universal, why not let the non-Christian peoples alone? Why is it necessary for Christians to do anything for them?" Such questions are illogical and arise simply from failure to realize that this modern view applies not simply to foreign missions, but to the activity of Christians at home and to all philanthropic and religious efforts of Christians anywhere.

Who doubts that God is doing all He can for every man in Christian America? But is that any reason why the activity of the churches, and the Young Men's Christian Associations, and the manifold organizations for the spiritual, social, and economic betterment of men in Christian lands should be given up? Is that a reason why parents need do nothing for the training of their children, or why all men are not under solemn obligations to God to do their best for neighbors and fellow-citizens and for all classes of the community at home? No one would claim this. The more that we are conscious of God's opening new opportunities to other men, and the more resources that He has given to any man, the more we recognize the responsibility of that man to God always to do his very best for every man. It is almost axiomatic that the man of many privileges who fails to recognize and meet his added responsibilities, thereby incurs added sin, and suffers that retribution which the Lord Jesus Christ said would always come upon those who fail to improve and to impart the privileges which their Heavenly Father has kindly given to them. "To whom much is given, of them much also will be required." When Peter first realized that God is no respecter of persons; but that "in every nation he that feareth Him and worketh righteousness is acceptable to Him," that did not make him think it needless to give the Christian message. It encouraged him in giving it. The same conviction should be to us what it was to Peter, an added reason for preaching Christ. Nor did the devout Cornelius on hearing this confession from Peter imagine that, because God accepts devout men of every faith, therefore he had no need of the Lord Jesus Christ. On the contrary, he the more promptly and quickly placed himself among the disciples of Christ. Such, also, is the ordinary experience of the devout non-Christian nowadays. It is not the broader and more Christian statement of God's attitude to devout men in other faiths which drives such men from God, but the narrower view, which belittles the spirit of the God who is pleased to recognize every aspiration and every obedience to Himself, whether men have received their inspiration directly from Jesus Christ or not.

I reserve for the sixth lecture the consideration of an additional gain to foreign missions from the modern view of God and the world, viz., the gain which is to come from missionary activity to Christian thought in lands now Christian, when peoples that are now non-Christian shall from their own view-points have accepted the Lord Jesus Christ as their Lord and spiritual helper.

"God sends His teachers unto every age,
To every clime and every race of men,
With revelations fitted to their growth
And shape of mind, nor gives the realm of truth
Unto the selfish rule of one sole race:
Therefore each form of worship that hath swayed
The life of man, and given it to grasp
The master-key of knowledge, reverence,
Infolds some germs of goodness and of right;
Else never had the eager soul, which loathes
The slothful down of pampered ignorance,
Found in it even a moment's fitful rest."

II

THE HISTORICAL DEVELOPMENT OF HINDUISM

NOWADAYS it is axiomatic that we know nothing thoroughly unless we know it historically. Especially if we wish to know any subject that is apart from us, it is important to know its history; how it came to be what it is. In order to know the ethnic religions aright we need to know them historically. As one contribution to such an effort, I offer a statement of how Hinduism came to be what it is. Hinduism is the religion of the Hindus. For the present object of these lectures, my definition of Hinduism is that it is the interpretation by the Hindus, in thought and practice, of what God has been trying to teach them about their relation to Himself and to their fellowmen. The many weaknesses and errors of Hinduism are due to the misapprehension by Hindus of the God who was ever seeking to reveal Himself to them, even while they were feeling after Him, if haply they could find Him. I believe that the statement which is now to be made is, in a large and general way, psychologically and chronologically correct. I would not claim more than that it is correct in a large and general way, for more information is likely to suggest some modifications in the description which is now made. But I believe that the religious literature of India, and the present condition of its multitudinous phases substantiate the positions taken.

Hinduism is not one homogeneous system. It is a conglomeration of beliefs and practices, many of which are inconsistent and contradictory. This is partly because different elements have gone to make up Hinduism, and very naturally in Hinduism, as in other religions, mutually inconsistent beliefs and practices have been followed by the masses without realizing that they were inconsistent. But the same phenomenon appears more or less in all the religions of the world, and in other spheres than the strictly religious. Hinduism is a mixture of inconsistent and contradictory beliefs and practices, partly because the Hindu mind has come to be so constituted that it is not critical and that it easily says "Yes" to almost anything which is presented to it. And, vice versa, the Hindu religion has helped to make the Hindu mind thus vague and in a way comprehensive. Some years ago I was asked to secure for publication in a magazine of the Chicago University, from some recognized Vaishnava authority in western India, a statement of the Vaishnava phase of Hinduism, *i. e.*, the sect of Hinduism which considers Vishnu as the chief god. In order to ascertain who would be regarded as such an authority on Vaishnavism I went to the most prominent and influential Hindu gentleman in western India, the Hon. Mahadev Govind Ranade, who was a Justice of the High Court in Bombay and long president of the Social Conference of India. When I told him what the Chicago University wished me to secure, Judge Ranade replied, "It is impossible for you or anyone to get a statement of any phase of Hinduism which would be entirely acceptable to anyone except the writer, because there is no one recognized statement of Hinduism, and no person authorized to make a complete statement of any phase of

Hinduism." However, with a good deal of difficulty I secured a statement which was submitted first to a Hindu professor of Sanskrit in the Deccan College, Poona, who was a professing Vaishnava. But before he was willing to give even a general sanction to the statement which had been submitted to him he consulted various Hindu shastris, *i. e.*, men learned in Hindu religious books. After such careful examination, when he returned the statement, he did not seem to feel that the paper was an exact statement of what it professed to be. Such an incident partly explains why different persons make different estimates of what Hinduism really is. Generalization is always dangerous without a very large basis of knowledge and experience, and even then only when made by a person of judicial mental habits. Mistaken estimates of Hinduism are very common, because generalizations about it have been made without adequate knowledge and without adequate recognition of the history of Hinduism. Some missionaries have unintentionally made erroneous, because too sweeping, statements of what Hinduism is, because they supposed that those phases of modern popular Hinduism with which they have come in contact among the lower classes—albeit those lower classes form a very large section of the community—were the whole of Hinduism. On the contrary, some Western visitors to India and some Hindu visitors to the West have made equally erroneous statements of what Hinduism is by too sweeping assumptions that the more spiritual conceptions of the philosophic books of the Hindus were the whole of the Hindu religion.

According to the definition of religion used in these lectures, if the religion of any people be taken as their interpretation of what God has been trying to teach them, then a correct statement of the Christian religion would not be a summary of the most spiritual teachings of Jesus Christ. It would be the interpretation in thought and in practice by the Christians in question of the teachings and person of Jesus Christ. Similarly, in a large and broad sense Hinduism is not the most spiritual conception of the most philosophic books. It is the interpretation by the Hindus from early times to the present of their relations to God and men.

In accordance with the modern view of God and the world, which was claimed in the former lecture as the true way for the wise missionary of these times to study Hinduism, I believe that a survey of how it has come to be what it is will show the goodness of God in seeking to reveal Himself to His Hindu children, while it will also show how sadly they have often misunderstood Him. Since God is light and in Him is no darkness at all, He Himself has always been wishing and trying to reveal Himself to His Hindu children as well as to His other children. In fact, it was because He was seeking them that they felt after Him. But even yet the Hindu has not adequately recognized that supreme characteristic of God which Jesus Christ revealed, viz., that God needs His human children, and so longs for them that He counts no sacrifice or effort too great to bring them all into intimate filial relations with Himself.

This study of the historic development of Hinduism will probably give another surprising revelation to some in Christian lands, viz., that just as no feature of the religious history of Israel is more characteristic and inspiring than the frequency with which protestant reformers, or prophets, came to protest against formality, injustice, and impurity among the Hebrews, and to call them back face to face with a righteous, living God, and thereby to strengthen them in trouble and to purify them, so in India there have been many protestants against the imperfections of current religious thought, and many theistic reformers of unsatisfactory living. Probably more protestant reformers have appeared in the religious history of India than in the religious history of Israel; perhaps more than in the Christian Church. While this statement may seem surprising to some, is it not what we should expect from such a living, righteous, spiritual, loving God, as has been revealed to us by Jesus Christ? The Lord Jesus never implied or said that God the Father of the spirits of all men had through what Jesus himself did or said become different from what He evermore had been and must be. Jesus Christ came to reveal the Father, not to make God a Father. "The only begotten Son, who is in the bosom of the Father, he hath revealed Him," not made him different. "He that hath seen the Son hath seen the Father," *i. e.*, hath seen God as He evermore is, not as He has become changed to be through Christ's revelation.

This study will also illustrate the correctness of the remark in a former lecture that one common weakness in the religion of any man or people consists in a mistake about proportion, in one-sidedness, in over-emphasis of one phase of truth and in neglect of other phases. It will also bring into new clearness and significance the fact that Jesus Christ is the one in whom the fullness of God dwells: and that as in the fullness of time twenty centuries ago He came to fulfill what was in the bud in the Judaic system, so in the present fullness of time for India He seeks to fulfill all partial and imperfect apprehensions of truth which in mixed measure or in great error have been perceived by the religious teachers of that country. Such a study will also bring into prominence the marvelous patience of God in dealing with His human children: a patience so beautifully expressed in the Biblical phrase, "With God a thousand years are as one day."

This delineation of the historical development

of Hinduism will also bring out the usual double tendency in thought and life everywhere—both the upward and the downward pull. What Paul taught on this point is the ordinary experience in all human nature; not only the human nature of the Jew and the Greek, but also of the Hindu. The spirit and the flesh are at enmity with one another. That is, God is ever trying to pull men up, and the lower elements of human nature are always trying to pull men away from God. Because the downward tendency often had temporary victory in Israel, God sent protestant reformers or prophets to that chosen people of His. So, because the downward tendency has been more characteristic of Hinduism than of the religion of Israel, God has sent protestant reformers to that people also. The higher the spiritual vision which was reached by any of the religious leaders and thinkers of India, the sadder the fruits of modern popular Hinduism appear in the well-nigh universal prevalence of idolatry, ignorance, superstition, and caste in that country, until the glorious Gospel of the blessed God as revealed in Jesus Christ has brought to that land its fullness of time and has begun to dissipate the darkness and error of modern popular Hinduism.

With these preliminary illustrations of what the history of Hinduism will illustrate, I now briefly state how Hinduism has come to be what it is, viz., a conglomerate or mixture of the different religious thoughts and practices of the Hindus for centuries. Without giving many explicit illustrations of the religious practices of Hindus, I shall speak briefly of those influences or ideas which have been formative, and which have been embodied in cultus, as well as in thought. Sometimes a succession of religious strata is recognizable, like geological strata on the surface of the earth. But because religion is a living thing, more often the different phases of life which have made up Hinduism have become very much intermingled. For this reason it is not now easy to distinguish the different elements.

In general, the hill tribes and low castes of India are largely the survivors of those people of Kolarian or Dravidian origin who inhabited India before the Aryans entered that land. In the religious thought and practices of these lower classes of the community we see a large measure of the earliest formative principle of what has brought about the huge religious mass now called the Hindu religion. That first formative principle was the principle of fear. Fear is a considerable part of the religion of many, perhaps of most, men in most religions. But certainly in the thought and practice of the lower classes in India fear easily was, and still is, the original and most essential principle; fear of the unknown, of the dark, because it includes the unknown; of dangerous places and dangerous animals; of unexplained and strange phenomena, such as eclipses, comets, etc.; fear of disease, of death, etc. As primitive Hindus came into contact with such phases of life they naturally wished and sought for escape from such fearful influences. And they sought to secure escape by propitiating the unknown and the terrible. Once as I was going for a tramp on a mountain range my guide said, "Before we start, let me go and make a vow to my god." I followed him, and after he had stood a moment under a sacred tree, I asked, "What did you vow?" He replied, "I vowed to hang a bell in the tree, if I should see no snake on this excursion." Snakes are the objects most feared in those hills, and the reason why, without understanding the real reason, he vowed to hang a bell in the branches was, no doubt, this: Snakes are afraid of noises. Therefore, whenever the wind shakes the tree and makes the bell tinkle, a snake dislikes to stay under that tree. So it is not strange that those rude and superstitious people vaguely connect a sacred tree having bells hanging in its branches with some power which helps to drive away snakes.

The second formative principle in the development of Hinduism came from the early immigrants of Aryan stock. It was principally the influence of the more helpful phases of Nature. This fact appears in the hymns of the Rig Veda. Songs, prayers, and offerings are made to the sky, sun, moon, dawn, woods, fire, rain, etc. This fact is so well known that illustrations from Vedic hymns are hardly needed. When those earliest Aryans came in contact with the dark-skinned Dravidians who were in the land before them, then that happened which usually happens when people of different religious ideas intermingle. The religion of the earlier people absorbed something from the brighter, the more cheerful thought of their Aryan masters, while the religion of the Aryans was also affected somewhat by the darker aspects of their servants' religion. Masters cannot help being influenced by the ideas and practices of servants, even as servants cannot help being influenced by the ideas and practices of their masters. However far one advances into the labyrinth of Hinduism, he always finds superstition, devils, demons, magic, witchcraft, and uncanny things, which are the earliest element of Hinduism surviving to the present day in the religion of a great many Hindus. Yet the brighter aspect of Nature, which was the special contribution of the primitive Aryans to Hinduism, has also had its part in making Hinduism what it is to-day. The justification of this position and an illustration of the mingling of these two elements can be given from the well-known fact that the Atharva Veda, which is later than the Rig Veda, has both the hymns of the Rig Veda and the magic and charms and maledictions which came from the first element of Hinduism. Superstition lingers very, very long in man, and even those who consider themselves most cultured and most philosophical in the most privileged sections of America still have many strange and injurious superstitions influencing them in thought and life.

As life became more complex and the roving companies of Aryans settled into community life, and society became more coherent, and the interests of different communities seemed to clash, and difficulties increased, a third formative influence came into the making of the religion of India. The characteristics of strong leaders of the community became more valued and more influential than the various aspects of physical Nature. Men of strength and courage were considered worthy of more honor. They were praised not only while alive, but after their death, and the apotheosis of former heroes became a prominent principle in the thought and life of the country. In all religions hero-worship has been a prominent and formative influence. In the period succeeding Vedic times hero-worship was the principal element in literature and in religion. It certainly was so in the epic poems which have exerted so great an influence in India, and it was so even in times earlier than the great epics.

But as life became still more complex, and as knowledge and skill naturally took precedence of physical force and courage, wise men became more and more influential, and the memories of wise men gone received more and more attention and became objects of reverence in the thought of the times. In no country has knowledge come to have the preëminence that it has had in India. There knowledge is the great thing. Nothing in Indian thought and life, neither money, material advantages, social prominence, nor political power, have ever been such objects of respect and desire as they are in the West. It is knowledge or wisdom which is the great thing. Even the rites and institutions of religion have been valued by the thoughtful in India not for their own sakes, but as the means of securing knowledge. And as knowledge came to have such a preëminence it grew into the belief that man's spirit is not only his chief element, is not mortal; it is a part of or is even identical with the universal and immortal. There was nothing too much to inquire into. Yet even in those times the teachers of India recognized some limitations to the understanding. In the Brihad Aranyaka Upanishad III. 6 after a pupil had over and over again pushed inquiries in ontology the teacher Yājñavalkya said, "Do not over-question lest your head fall off. In truth you are over-questioning a divinity about which further questions cannot be asked." There are two results of this kind of thinking. One result was the feeling that nothing is real: that life is not worth living. In other words, the first result was pessimism. It was just the result which came to the thinker in Ecclesiastes, "Vanity of vanities; all is vanity." The other result was that the thinkers knew, and plain men knew, that this kind of philosophy was of no use for the masses; and so endless rites and meaningless ceremonies were placed upon the common crowd, which came to be a yoke that pressed most sorely upon their hearts and lives.

So, while search by the intellect for a better understanding of the inward meaning of religion was an upward response to what God was trying to teach the Hindus, yet in this connection there developed one of the greatest dangers to true religion, viz., pride of intellect and contempt of common men. The thinkers sought to spin out their speculation finer and finer, but they did not consider how they could better help their less cultivated fellowmen. They sought knowledge only for itself. For the masses they formed an exoteric system of rituals and sacrifices, and for the initiated an esoteric system. While theoretically rites and sacrifices were elevated into usage only for the common people, the priests and teachers themselves fell into the practice because they could not command such practices on the masses without themselves taking a part in what they commanded. The word Yoga, meaning "union," is a principal word at this time, and Yoga as both the aim and the means of union with the divine was made to consist largely in terrible austerities. Religion became mainly a yoke of ceremonies and formulas, beginning for the individual before he was born and continuing for two or three generations in his family after he had left this world. The object of Yoga was not to develop into their fullest exercise the natural powers of body and mind, and all the sweet relations of human society, but to restrict and put them away. The result was disastrous in two directions. It was disastrous for the thinkers, because it displaced simple and natural living by formal introspection. It was disastrous for the masses, because religion was thought to consist in meaningless and formal external acts. The thinker went into pantheism; not into recognition of a personal God, but of an impersonal chain of events, in which the doctrine of *Karma* made the whole course of life here and hereafter one of fate. Pride of intellect always injures both heart and will. It caused coldness of heart among the leaders of the Hindu religion. Instead of inspiring the leaders to instruct and uplift the masses, it made them mislead the masses with set purpose. The priests became unscrupulous, selfish, and greedy; and formalism resulted in hypocrisy, as it always must with intelligent men. Meanwhile ceaseless and meaningless rites turned the religion of the masses also into formalism, which is the first great bane of religion. So, whereas the fuller use of the intellect should have diminished the principle of fear in the religion of the Hindus, formalism and sacerdotalism wrought the very opposite result. For now it was not only fear of the unknown in men's immediate surroundings for this world, but fear of the unknown future which became the most influential motive in the religion of the people. The common people were afraid of their religious leaders. The curse of an ascetic was supposed to cause unavoidable and irresistible injury in this world and the next. Sin was not principally unethical conduct, but the omission of ceremonials and the disregard of custom. The only possible expiation for such sin was not in true repentance and a better life, but in the heaviest mortifications, in piling up good deeds to overcome demerit. Also, because the masses could not understand nor accept pantheism pure and simple, its logical opposite, viz., polytheism, came into common acceptance. This is the nemesis which may always be expected for pride and selfishness. The All-god, or It, could be recognized by the common people only in its partial presence in manifold forms and places. Therefore many gods in many sacred places came to be worshiped by the common people.

But despite this new misreading of God's intention, He was still working to reveal Himself to His Hindu children, and the next upward movement was one which emphasized the more spiritual truth that not knowledge, but goodness and helpfulness to brother-men, is the great thing in religion. This first great protestant reformation in India came through Siddartha, or Gautama, who became the Buddha, or "enlightened one." He was a contemporary of that Isaiah who was the most inspired and inspiring prophet in the latter part of the Babylonish captivity. As the great prophet of the captivity under the inspiration of God brought to the people of Israel in their decline a protest against formality, injustice, and unbrotherliness, and taught that God could be pleased by nothing save righteous living, so by God's help Siddartha became the enlightened one and similarly protested against formality and unbrotherliness among the Hindus. As a protestant against the burdensome religion of the Brahman priests the Buddha became an apostle of the simple and pure life. He protested against the uselessness and the harm of formality. He preached the necessity and value of kindness, gentleness, and purity. He came in "a fullness of time"; for caste had become a tremendous burden on the social system and was injuring both the upper and the lower classes by increasing pride and hard feelings. The people were ripe for a more human system, and the caste system which Brahmanism had made so burdensome was largely modified by Buddha and his followers. The tyranny of a religion consisting of meaningless ceremonies was largely put away, and a more simple religion of kindness and purity supplanted the religion of the Brahmans. The new system gradually developed into the Buddhism which we know.

But, though Buddha was enlightened on some very fundamental points, he did not apprehend, as the great prophet of Israel did, the most important of all points, viz., that ethical culture could not take the place of loyalty to a personal God. Practically Buddha had nothing to say about God at all, so that strictly he was not atheistic, but non-theistic in his teachings and influence. However, though he did not say anything about a personal God, yet his own personality was probably the principal inspiration which gave force and permanence to his teachings. His example and life are even to this day considered by devout Buddhists as the principal attraction of men. Buddha himself became practically deified. By the impulse of his teachings and life for nearly a thousand years Buddhism supplanted Brahmanism. This spread and development of Buddhism also depended a good deal upon political power and circumstances. For in about three hundred years after Buddha's time the great emperor Ashoka adopted the Buddhist faith, gathered councils to unify and consolidate the teachings of Buddhism, built buildings for it, caused important inscriptions to be cut on various monuments, sent out missionaries, and gave Buddhism a prevalence which it probably would not otherwise have secured. However, in the lapse of time several great changes came over the simplicity of the religion which Gautama had taught. Veneration for him extended to articles and places with which he had been connected.

His images were made and scattered all over the land. Such reverence soon developed into idolatry. While idols are not referred to in the Rig Veda, it is most probable that some places and objects had been practically worshiped from the earliest times by the most backward classes. But later Buddhism increased idolatry more than any other influence in India, and the substitution of rites and ceremonies obscured the spiritual light which God had revealed through Buddha, and Buddhism, too, became largely a formal religion.

In this connection a brief statement should be made about a movement closely allied to Buddhism, which started at about the same time and which has had some survival to the present, viz., the Jain revival. It was at first both an ethical and intellectual revolt against the ritualism and pantheism of the preceding period when that phase of Hinduism called Brahmanism was in the ascendency. Mahavira, the reputed founder of Jainism, like Buddha, was of royal birth. Unlike Buddha, the metaphysics which he taught was a sort of dualism, a distinction between the individual spirit and the world spirit. It started with making the three gems of religion to be right knowledge, right intuition, right life. Like Buddhism, but with greater emphasis, Jainism has placed special emphasis on the doctrine of non-injury to all life, even to the humblest insect life. But like Buddhism, Jainism has gradually given more and more emphasis to the importance of asceticism for the professedly religious class, has developed monastic institutions, has developed degrading views of reincarnation and hell, and made, not the good of others, but the suppression of the normal powers of mind and body the principal thing in religion; while for the common classes to eat and enjoy in this life became the essence of religion. But Jainism has had little practical influence on the religious thought of India. At present it has become a religion in which the chief points are the practical denial of a personal God; reverence amounting to worship of the high priests of the religion; and the nourishing of vermin and other lower forms of animal life. So for both Buddhism and Jainism the old story has been repeated. The spiritual sense of their worshipers became dulled, formalism took a new lease of life, and the ceremonies and superstitions of Hinduism prior to the Buddhistic reformation returned. The evil spirit which had been cast out came back with seven other spirits worse than itself.

After the Buddhist period the man who for the thinking class brought about the revival of Hindu Pantheism was the greatest modern Hindu religious teacher, Shankarāchārya. In the ninth century A.D. he developed Hindu thought into a well-ordered pantheistic system by his commentaries on the Vedanta Sutra. But the Hinduism of the period from the ninth century onward was still a conglomerate, heterogeneous mass of elements drawn from the religion of the aborigines, where fear was the formative principle; from the Vedic period, where the brighter aspects of nature were more formative; from the post-Vedic period, when hero-worship had large influence; from the Upanishad period when reverence for knowledge was considered still higher; and from the Buddhist revival, when goodness and helpfulness to men were considered more truly what religion rightly is. However, the flesh had again won the victory over the spirit; and now not only was formality in the ascendant, but even immorality, and sometimes bestiality, came into great prominence in the religion of India. Scholars truly say that the literature of India is so largely a mixture of newer additions and interpolations with the older strata that it is difficult to distinguish the different elements. But certainly after the decline of Buddhism polytheism (with a sub-stratum of pantheism), idolatry, and caste, came to be the controlling elements in popular Hinduism. Even gods were represented as in many respects immoral. This interpretation was doubtless due in considerable measure to the literalizing of language which was originally figurative, though sensuous. Thus the older and more spiritual Krishna of the Bhagavad Gita became the immoral Krishna of the later stories. The Manes or departed spirits became semi-deified. By sacrifices and austerities priests and holy men came to be thought to possess power at which the gods trembled. The gods tried to entice holy men into sin. Personified Fate was the mightiest of powers. The sacred books describe the downward course of religious life by the universal recognition of the four ages as Krita, Treta, Dvāpāra, and Kali, corresponding to the classic descent from the golden to the iron age; the present being the Kali, or the sinful age. Every Hindu reformer makes the same assertion, that the present state of religion in India is that of a sad decline. In this depraved condition the Purānas are the literature which exhibit Hinduism at its lowest level. They are full of exaggerations, miracles, and puerilities. Some of these taught a somewhat spiritual interpretation. But others taught very unworthy doctrines. Where any altruistic regard for the good of fellowmen prevailed, there was some response to the upward drawing of God. Where only selfish considerations prevailed, there the tendency was toward both superstition and immorality. Thus most of the sects of modern Hinduism have what are called a right-hand and a left-hand phase. The left-hand phase is confessedly immoral. In general, the sects of Shaivism, *i. e.*, those who regard Shiva as the great god, have the grosser and more despicable characteristics, while the sects of Vaishnavism, that is those who regard Vishnu as the great god, are with some exceptions of a less unworthy character. Among other debasing characteristics Shiva was considered the god of thieves; and many unworthy beliefs and practices come under the head of Shaivism. Probably the most immoral and sensual sect of Vaishnavism is that of the Vallabhas which is found especially in Bombay and Kutch. Their spiritual leaders, entitled Maharajas, are considered incarnations of God and command the absolute devotion of their followers. Their worship is often erotic and immoral in tendency. But the downward tendency of popular religion is especially seen in its worst phase as described in the late books called the "Tantras." Here are stated in some detail some of the secret practices of that large branch of modern popular Hinduism denominated Shāktas, *i. e.*, those who especially worship *shakti*, the female principle. That I may not perhaps be thought to make an over-statement, I will quote from Prof. E. W. Hopkins, the successor of Prof. W. D. Whitney and the present professor of Sanskrit in Yale University: "Obscenity is the soul of this cult.

. . . In practice, Shakti-worship, when unveiled, amounts to this: that men and women of the same class and family indulge in a Bacchanalian orgy, and that, as they proceed, they give themselves over to every excess which liquor and lust can promote. A description of the different rites would be to reduplicate an account of indecencies of which the least vile is too esoteric to sketch faithfully. Vaguely to outline one such religious festival will suffice. A naked woman, wife of the chief priest, sits in the middle of the 'holy circle.' She represents Durga, the divine female principle. The Bacchic orgy begins with hard drinking. Shiva as Bhairava, the 'dreadful,' has his human counterpart also, who must then and there pair with the impersonated Durga. The worship proper consists in a repetition of numerous *mantra* syllables and yells; the worship improper, in indulgence in wine and women (particularly enjoined in books called Tantras). Human sacrifices at these rites are said to be extinct at the present day. But blood lust is appeased by the hacking of their own bodies. Garments are cast in a heap and lots are drawn for the women's garments by the men. With her whose clothes he gets each man continues the debauch, inviting incest in addition to all other excess."

But while all this degrading movement was going on in a considerable part of Hinduism, the living God was not leaving himself without witness, even as Paul said to the men of Lystra. In the latter half of the fifteenth century, in the northwestern part of India, God raised up a reformer named Chaitanya, who was a contemporary of Luther. Like Luther, he, too, protested against the doctrine of salvation by meritorious deeds and austerities. He preached salvation by *bhakti*, that is by trustful adoration of God. Like most religious reformers in India he also protested against caste. It was in some measure the counterpart of the reformation in Germany led by Luther, in which salvation, not by merit, but by faith, was the spiritual truth which brought about the great Protestant Reformation of Christianity. Chaitanya's doctrine of salvation by *bhakti*—or the devotion of love—was, however, expressed in sensuous language which is common to religion in India. It was represented that the devotee should feel toward God such affection as a young man feels for a young woman. Yet probably Chaitanya himself meant by these words not any physical or sensual affection. He taught the value of singing and dancing and other outward means of arousing the religious fervor which would express *bhakti* or love to God. But, whereas Chaitanya began with spiritual principles, his followers soon fell into quarrels and fanaticism and even immorality. And a new illustration occurred of the power of the flesh to quench the spirit.

I return now to another means which God used to remind men of Himself, and which was a protest against polytheism, idolatry, and caste, which three elements have always been the bane of all unsound religious teaching in India. Chronologically this new influence began earlier than the later phases of Hinduism which have just been described. It came through the contact of Islam with India. This religion of the Mohammedans who conquered northern India was not Mohammedanism at its best; but it had some pure and strong features. It passionately emphasized monotheism, and the folly and wrong of idolatry. In many places this passion was exhibited by the breaking of idols, the disfiguring of Hindu temples, and the sequestering of the endowment of priests and temples. Certain Mohammedan kings, notably Akbar the Just, who invited Hindus to his court and gave them opportunity to study other faiths and to influence one another, exercised a liberalizing influence on Hinduism. In various ways the influence of the monotheism and the spiritual worship of Islam led many thinkers in northern India to give up pantheism and idolatry. Yet the Hindu type of monotheism among Hindu reformers was a distinctively different type from the monotheism of the Mohammedans. Hindu monotheism recognized the immanence of one God in His universe, as the distinctive God of Islam never was thought to abide in men. One of the most valuable results of such an historical study of the development of the religion of India is the clear fact that, as different changes came about, the Hindus modified, but never broke away from, their past religious inheritance. The influence of Mohammedanism was really considerable, for God used Islam as the chief stimulus to new protestant reformers in India. One of the most prominent of these was Kabir, who probably lived in the early part of the fifteenth century. He powerfully assailed polytheism and idolatry, ridiculed the authority of the sacred books, and taught that the spirit is the only authority in religion. But there appeared in him and in his followers that same lack of balance and consistency which has made many spiritual reforms largely valueless. He eventually had an apotheosis. His disciples required such obedience to him as made him almost a deity. Even now in western and northern India one comes across followers of Kabir, who quote admirable spiritual sentiments from their teacher of five centuries ago. Later in the fifteenth century in the Panjab, where Mohammedanism has come into closest contact with Hinduism, God raised up another protestant reformer, Nānak, the first acknowledged founder of the Sikh religion. The word " Sikh " exactly means " disciple." The controlling principles of the Sikh religion were, as most reforms in later times have been, protests against pantheism, polytheism, idolatry, formality, injustice, and caste. The protests of the prophets of Israel were largely directed against the very same evils, and the teaching of Nānak and his successors, notably Arjun and Guru Govind Singh, were collected in a sacred book or "Granth." The spiritual power of this purer religion made the Sikhs a militant body which became a most powerful political force in the Panjab. Guru Govind instituted the worship of the sword and the book. But though this religious reformation received its initial inspiration from Islam, it remained truly Indian. The Sikhs never became Mohammedans; on the contrary, they fought them. However, starting with a spiritual religion and with some degree of brotherhood, the Sikhs have degenerated into formality. While rejecting the Vedas and caste, they practically worship the various gods of the Hindus. They even worship the Granth, *i. e.*, their sacred book, with incense and offerings, which is the regular Hindu worship of idols. It is a closed book which they worship. Sikhism, like Islam, being the religion of a book, has ceased to be a growing religion, and is therefore a decaying religion. So certainly is Sikhism a dying religion that recently an appeal was made to the British government of India to do something to revive Sikhism, on the plea that if the religion which had made the Sikhs a fighting people and loyal to rulers should die, then the militant spirit would die out in the race which has supplied splendid fighters for the British army. More conclusive evidence that Sikhism is a dying religion could not be given than such an appeal for help from the secular power of a Christian king. In the sixteenth century another great reformer named Dādu arose in the Northwest, where Mohammedanism had been influential. Dādu, too, emphasized monotheism, the spiritual worship of God, and the evil of caste. Some of his teachings are of a high spiritual order. He emphasized the immanence and love of God, and taught that salvation consists in goodness. But as usual among Hindus, his followers have split up into a great many subdivisions and fallen into much formality. In the seventeenth century other reforming sects arose, such as the Bābalas and the Sādhus; in the eighteenth century the Satnāmis, *i. e.*, worshipers of the true name.

At last I turn to the influence of Christianity on the religious development of India. Though some claim that centuries ago Christianity had some considerable influence in modifying Hinduism, I am strongly of the opinion that this is a strained and mistaken inference. There are some resemblances between some stories of Krishna and some events in the life of Christ. But these have not been borrowed on either side. They are independent and accidental resemblances which really show the difference between the two stories. The most influential and fair-minded Indian scholar on these subjects, Prof. R. G. Bhandarkar, told me that this is his impression also. Similarly, it has been thought that the Hindu triad or *trimurtti*, which seems unquestionably to be rather a late idea of Hinduism, was suggested by the Christian doctrine of the Trinity. To me this seems very unlikely. Early in the Christian era a branch of the Christian Church undoubtedly found some lodgment in India. At least in the sixth century, A.D., there was a Christian Church in Malabar, on the southwestern coast of India. But it has had little effect on Hindu thought and life. Two hundred years ago the Roman Catholic Church sent missionaries into India, who have secured many followers, and about a century ago Christian Protestants began to send missionaries there. The numerical result of these two missionary efforts is a Christian community of about three million people. But it is freely admitted by many of the most intelligent reformers and thinkers of India that the Christian thought which has recently come to India has powerfully affected many religious movements which do not take the Christian name. The most important, though not the most numerous, of these reform movements, which though not calling itself Christian is very considerably Christian in thought and spirit, is the Brahma Samāj, or theistic church of India. By the express admission of its leaders God inspired this important reforming and spiritual movement largely through the teachings and life of Jesus Christ. The history of this Brahma Samāj is so well known that it needs little enlargement from me. In the early part of the nineteenth century Rammohun Roy became an ardent student of all the religions of the world.

In 1820 he wrote a book called the "Precepts of Jesus," and organized a distinct theistic movement which accepted a modified pantheism, which gave great value to the spiritual teachings of all religions, and which modified caste. Then that happened to this movement which happens to all reforms, viz., conflict between the conservative and progressive elements. The progressive element wished to give greater prominence to Jesus Christ and still more to modify caste, while the conservatives held back. This caused a split. The conservative element retained the name of the Adi Samāj, *i. e.*, the original church, and the progressives were known as the Brahma Samāj. Again conflict arose between the conservative and the progressive elements. Then the progressives, under the greatest of modern religious reformers in India, Keshab Chundar Sen, went out to form a new theistic body which took the name of the "New Dispensation," while the conservatives retained the name of "Sādhāran Brahma Samāj," or "middle church." Again, at the death of Keshab Chundar Sen a new split arose in the New Dispensation, the progressive element being led by Keshab's great lieutenant, Pratap Chundar Moozumdar. In western India a corresponding theistic movement, which refuses to ally itself with the Brahma Samāj of Bengal, is called the Prārthanā Samāj, *i. e.*, "the prayer church." On the whole, the Brahma Samāj and the Prārthanā Samāj are very similar to the Unitarian Church of the West. In the Panjab another reforming movement is called the Arya Samāj. It has come less under the influence of Christianity and harks back more to the purer early phases of Hinduism. But undoubtedly it is Christianity which has made the Arya Samāj come into existence and which has powerfully influenced it. New religious sects largely influenced by Christianity are springing up all over the country. One Hindu thinker in Ceylon has written commentaries on the Gospels of St. Matthew and St. John, and it is a common admission by Hindu thinkers and in Hindu newspapers that India reverences the Lord Jesus. Some frankly call Him easily the greatest of spiritual gurus; others call Him one of the greatest spiritual gurus of the world. Keshab Chundar Sen said, "It is Christ who rules British India, not the British government. . . . None but Christ; none but Christ; none but Christ hath deserved this bright, this precious diadem, India, and Jesus shall have it."

The value of such a survey of the historic development of religion in India ought to be manifold. It ought to make God seem very great, very near, and very active in the minds and lives of all men, as the modern Christian view requires us to believe. This survey also shows how great is the downward pull of the lower elements of human nature. Yet it shows that, however low people may go, God does not cease His efforts to draw them upward to Himself. It shows the awful fate which pantheism brings upon the intellectual and moral life of a people by weakening or denying all moral distinctions. Pantheism weakens both the mental and ethical powers of men. By its doctrine of illusion it creates lack of confidence in the reliability of all phenomena and mental conclusions. This survey also shows how polytheism always follows pantheism, how polytheism deadens the spirit, and how ritualism does the same. It shows the nemesis which follows Vedantic pantheism when ideas are substituted for ideals. Modern popular Hinduism also shows how dangerous it is when emotion and passion rule without intellectual restraint and easily run into immorality. In the case of all reformers and especially in the case of the great Buddha there is an illustration of the importance of the personal element in a religious leader, when example is joined to, and illustrates high teaching. There is also illustration of the entire inadequacy of ethical teaching to retain ethical purity apart from consistent recognition of God. The survey shows how comparatively little is the permanent influence of the thinker or the sage who lives for himself and for thought apart from the world. It shows how easily the common people fall into credulity and superstition and formality. A right understanding of this survey shows that despite God's patient teaching "by divers portions, in divers manners," certainly India has not yet come into a sense of filial relation to God and of the brotherhood of men. This one simple, undeniable, historical fact is enough of itself to show that India needs, and must have, the help of the Lord Jesus Christ in order to grow into that consciousness of filial relation to God and of brotherly relations to men which is the supreme revelation of Jesus Christ and the supreme achievement to which He inspires men. The survey shows that despite contracted views of God and of the Christian religion, it is only Christianity which has gone to India in a fraternal spirit of self-sacrifice to help men there. The survey, rightly understood, shows that, since God has long been doing a preparatory work, it is now *a priori* reasonable to recognize that the "fullness of time" has come for India, when God will, through Jesus Christ, give that land the same spiritual vision and power which He has given to western people. It shows that Christ is now powerfully influencing the religious thought of India. The survey also shows, what has not always been recognized, that it is not to be expected that Indians will wholly cut loose from their old national ways of thinking, even when they become Christians. They will have the characteristic Indian way of Christian thought and life. Just as in apostolic times the Jews who became Christians had still their Jewish type of Christianity, and the Greeks who became Christians developed a characteristic type of Christianity, and the Romans who became Christians developed a Roman type of Christianity, so Indian Christians will develop an Indian type of Christianity under the influence of the Lord Jesus Christ. It is very important for the Christian missionary to recognize this teaching of history, so that while he makes Jesus Christ known to India, like John the Baptist he may himself decrease and Jesus Christ increase in making Indian Christians of an Indian type. But this view of God's way of doing things makes it none the less, but more, the duty and the privilege of Christians in Christian lands from a sense of brotherhood to do all that they can promptly to give to India, in the best way, that knowledge of Jesus Christ which is the supreme blessing which God the Father of all men has given to Christendom, and has in reserve for all His children.

III

MISSIONS AND PSYCHOLOGY

IN the early years of foreign missionary effort a common, though unreal, picture represented the missionary as wearing a tall hat and a dress coat, standing under a palm tree, with a book in his hand, and talking to a company of half-clad savages crouching around and gazing at him in wonder. Before he went abroad the advice sometimes given to him as sound was, "Beware of the man of one book," meaning that a man who could easily quote the Bible from any place between its covers was the man who was thereby mighty in saving souls. The Bible without note or comment was thought to be the very best thing to place in the hands of anyone whom it was sought to lead to Christ.

Things are different now. It is admitted to be of great importance that a wise missionary ought to know with some degree of fullness and accuracy the history of the development of religion among the people to whom he goes with the Christian message. It is admitted as equally important that he should have some careful and exact insight into the mind and characteristics of that people, and the ways in which their minds work. If knowledge of the history of every undertaking is important for the leader in spiritual work in America, even more so is knowledge of that branch of history which is termed Psychology: *i. e.*, knowledge of the way in which the minds of men have worked and now work. Therefore, psychology is coming to be considered necessary for wise work by any man among men in America. It is essential in pedagogy. It is important for parents in order adequately to meet their responsibilities. It is important for every minister to fit him to meet his responsibilities. James' suggestive book, "Varieties of Religious Experience," well points out how varied are the workings of different types of mind even in America. If psychology is important to any man for work among men of his own race, how much more important that he should understand the ways in which the minds of those of other races work, whose heredity and environment are different. Therefore, an understanding of general and universal psychological principles and particular psychological study of the peoples among whom the missionary works are of very great importance to every wise and strong teacher of Christianity in other lands. While this statement would *a priori* be accepted as presumptively true, experience confirms the statement. It is an everyday matter for people in India to say that foreign missionaries do not thoroughly understand them. Of course there is some real ground for such a statement. On the other hand, it is easy to over-state such a point. In some circles in the West it is almost a fad to claim that the differences between the Oriental and Occidental mind are so deep and numerous that it is almost hopeless for a man from the West really to understand the man from the East. Vice versa, it is as important to appreciate that human nature is essentially one in all the world, and that the human mind works on similar lines in every land and race, as to appreciate that there are differences in the working of minds of different races. The two foci of psychological truth are, first, that there are certain universal psychological laws; and, second, that there are diversities of mental characteristics in different races and in different individuals. The activities of the human mind are "diverse as the billows, yet one as the sea." Those who would over-emphasize the differences in the working of the Oriental and Occidental mind like to quote the lines of Kipling,

> "O! the East is East, and the West is West;
> And never the twain shall meet."

But they do not at the same time continue to quote the whole stanza, which is,

> "O! the East is East, and the West is West;
> And never the twain shall meet,
> Till earth and sky stand presently
> Before God's judgment seat.
> But there is neither East nor West,
> Nor border, nor breed, nor birth,
> When two strong men stand face to face,
> Though they come from the ends of the earth."

However like or unlike to ours the mental ways of men in other lands may be, it is unquestionably desirable for the foreign missionary to seek to know well the mental constitution of those with whom and for whom he works. The very effort to understand them will promote insight, sympathy, respect, and adaptation. And the greater the understanding and adaptation, the more will be the sympathy and respect. In other words, just as it is important and helpful to know the general religious condition of the country through knowing the historical development of its religion, so it is important and helpful to know the religious condition of individuals in that country by understanding the working of the minds of men of that type. Accordingly it is a legitimate compliment to missionaries of the past that, though psychology was a subject unknown in the curriculum of school, college, and theological seminary in their time, yet through genuine sympathy with the peoples among whom they worked and through high intelligence they had a fair understanding of the mental characteristics of those peoples. Travelers and scientists have often recorded their obligations to missionaries for helpful and accurate descriptions of the peoples among whom they had worked.

One of the benefits of psychological study to the missionary will be that he will not expect people in other lands to appreciate points which they are not accustomed to notice or value. Thus he will save them and himself much annoyance and disappointment. The teacher of Christianity has often perplexed men by raising points which are of no importance to them. In his "Varieties of Religious Experience" James makes a useful suggestion in pointing out that any theologian who spends needless time in describing attributes of God which have no definite connection with life, are not only undertaking what is needless, but are confusing and troublesome. He says for example, "God's personality apart from the moral qualities which it may comfort; his relations to evil being permissive and not positive; his self-sufficiency; self-love and absolute felicity in himself: candidly speaking, how do such qualities as these make any connection with our life? And if they severally have no distinctive adaptations of our conduct, what vital difference can it possibly make to a man's religion whether they be true or false? For my own part, although I dislike to say aught that may grate upon tender associations, I must frankly confess that though these attributes were faultlessly deduced, I cannot conceive of its being of the smallest consequence to us religiously that any one of them should be true. Pray, what specific act can I perform in order to adapt myself the better to God's simplicity? Or how does it assist me to plan my behavior, to know that his happiness is anyhow absolutely complete? . . . Surely the systematic theologians are the closet-naturalists of the diety. . . . What is their deduction of metaphysical attributes but a shuffling and matching of pedantic dictionary adjectives, aloof from morals, aloof from human needs, something that might be worked out from the mere word 'God' by one of those logical machines of wood and brass which recent ingenuity has contrived, as well as by a man of flesh and blood." When theologians in America have not distinguished essentials from non-essentials and from the many adjuncts of the Christian religion, and on account of denominational proclivities and jealousies have often raised even departures from essential Christianity into excessive prominence, it would be natural for the American theologian who goes to foreign lands to make the same mistake. If he did not appreciate how such points would only perplex the minds of men unused to such logic, he could not appreciate how misleading such a course would be. For example, how confusing and even grotesque to the Hindu or Japanese must be the giving of any importance to the various phases of Presbyterianism, such as Presbyterian, United Presbyterian, Reformed Presbyterian, Presbyterian North, Presbyterian South, Free Church Presbyterian, Established Church Presbyterian, "Wee-Free" Presbyterian, and the like. And if, in their simplicity and mental weakness, Christian adherents of missionaries of these various schools of Presbyterianism should accept these distinctions as important, how injurious to the simplicity that is in Christ Jesus would be the effect of such indigestible and strange teaching.

When I speak of Psychology and Missions some of the points which will be raised may not be considered by experts in the science as strictly psychological at all, when that science is defined as mainly a knowledge of the contents and working of consciousness as such. In general I shall speak of some of the mental characteristics of the Indian mind. I wish it to be distinctly understood that in the characterization which I make I am speaking only in general terms. I believe the following statements to be accurate in general, though some persons who are acquainted with India might make somewhat different characterizations and estimates of the Indian mind and its ways of working.

The first remark is that the Oriental mind is in many respects the type of mind of children in the West: less logical and more simple. Also the Indian mind is what it has come to be under the influence of race, climate, social conditions, and religious teaching and practices. These various influences have acted and reacted, so that it is not only difficult, but impossible, wholly to distinguish cause from effect. Social conditions have varied religion, and religion has affected social conditions. Climatic influences have helped to make the working of the Hindu mind not energetic, but languid. The same influences have made it easy to live without making practical considerations as controlling as in colder lands and less bountiful climates.

Many hard experiences from frequent famines and extreme poverty, and from being conquered by foreigners, have made the Hindu patient, as well as mild. Pantheism, with its injurious doctrine of illusion, denying the real existence of anything, has affected Hindus of all classes. It has weakened confidence in the reality of mental and moral, as well as outward, phenomena. In my opinion it is probably the Indian type of pantheism more than anything else which has caused those characteristics of the Hindu which have given him the reputation of not being truthful. The influence of the doctrine of illusion would naturally be the conviction that there is no need of accuracy of statement, or justification for aiming to be accurate. Another reason for the belief that truthfulness is not characteristic of the Hindu is more complimentary to the Hindu's heart than to the Hindu's mind. This reason is that the Hindu is so courteous and so anxious to avoid saying things which, though true, would be distasteful to the hearer, that he says things which, though inaccurate, will please his hearers. In other words, he prizes courtesy more than accuracy. This is a characteristic very objectionable to the westerner, who prizes truth and accuracy more than anything else. But popular Hinduism, as well as pantheism, has had an influence in weakening the Hindu's respect for truth. The later Hindu books have much to say about casuistry, and the circumstances under which lying is justifiable. Moreover, the very large use of figurative language largely accounts for what seems to the Occidental a very serious and grotesque departure from truth. Whereas such language is not understood by the people using it as meaning all that the words on their face would make an Occidental suppose they meant. This powerful imagination is both a weak and a strong point in the Indian mind. It makes the Indian less fitted to cope with all phases of life. It makes him satisfied with the unreal. On the other hand, who does not consider a strong imagination one of the most precious gifts of childhood? What added joy and value it gives to slender possessions! How much of the riches of literature comes from an exuberant imagination! How much of the satisfaction of parents, and especially of mothers, comes from fond imaginings about the future of their children! Imagination is the eye of faith which sees the invisible and which gives substance to hope. How large a part of Christian thinking and poetry depend on realizing God and heaven and future blessings through the imagination! The missionary to India needs thoroughly to understand and to appreciate how imagination is the most characteristic feature of the Indian mind.

Closely allied to this is another characteristic of the Hindu mind, in which it differs from the type of the adult male mind in the West. Men in the West ask for logic or proofs. The Indian cares little for logical evidence. What he wants is the conclusiveness of an illustration or a simile. Herein lies both a mental weakness and a mental strength. It is a weakness because it is easy in India, as elsewhere, to give an illustration more evidential value than it really has. Because a thing has once been so-and-so, it does not follow that it will be so again in the same department, much less that it will be so in another department. But to the Hindu it seems entirely conclusive to say that, just as there are many roads leading to a city, so there are many roads which lead to God. Logically this by no means follows. So if a Hindu knows that you once gave a man a certain present, he easily thinks you will do the same thing for him at any time. Like children, they cannot see that circumstances may be so different that you cannot, or that for some good reason you should not, do the same thing for him which you did for the other man. However, such valuation of an illustration more than of syllogistic proof gives useful working power to the Hindu mind, which if understood and rightly used may be very helpful to the missionary in his work. As a matter of fact, the larger part of mankind is rightly influenced more by the power of illustration than by a logical process of reasoning. How much of logic did Jesus Christ use? Very, very little. He stated the truth which He knew, and which He wished men to apprehend and follow, and often by illustrations of some kind enforced His teachings. His characteristic teaching by parables is essentially teaching by illustration and not by logic. The missionary from the West mistakes when he over-estimates the necessity or importance of logical proof in setting forth Jesus Christ and His teachings. For years after I became a missionary in India I supposed it necessary to *prove* the truth of Christianity. Nowadays I do not attempt that. I only seek to help men to see Christ as He was and spoke and is, *i. e.*, I try to exhibit His excellence, His betterness, His way of life. Experience shows this to be the most successful and satisfactory way. Even in America when the preacher follows Christ as his master in the way of teaching spiritual truth, as well as in accepting His interpretation of spiritual things, he will not attempt to prove things about Christ and His way. He will set Christ forth, will interpret His teachings and life in the vital and simple language of the times, and to such a message he will get a more satisfactory response. Nor do I try to prove the truth of the Bible any more than the truth of my mother, or wife, or children. I show the excellence of the Bible. That is not only enough; it is the satisfactory way for the majority of people in the West as well as in the East. In contrast with the logical methods of the West even the logical methods of the Hindus show how the latter values the illustration more than formal proofs. The syllogism of the West consists of three propositions: the major premise, the minor premise, and the conclusion. The syllogism of the Indian consists of five propositions: (1) the statement, or proposition; (2) the major premise; (3) the illustration; (4) the minor premise; and (5) the conclusion. The first, that is, the statement or proposition, is simply the conclusion, with which the syllogism is to close; yet the formal stating of it has an illustrative value to the Indian. In fact, a similar procedure is not very uncommon in the West, though books on logic say that the syllogism consists of three, and only three, members. We here do not make the proposition or conclusion the first step of our syllogistic process because it is not necessary, and the practical West takes the short cut to things, omitting needless steps. The Hindu syllogism has for its third member the illustration, which, as human nature goes, is really the conclusive element in most arguments, despite the fact that often the illustration may not be wholly pertinent or wholly parallel with the proposition which it seeks to establish. Many theologians in the West now definitely say that it is both useless and impossible to try to prove the existence of God because we practically assume Him before we try to deduce His existence by a syllogistic process.

An allied characteristic of the Hindu mind is the seemingly illogical way in which, while the doctrine of illusion makes real existence unreal, the doctrine of faith makes unrealities real. A common teaching of the religious books of India, and one of the commonest assumptions of ordinary men in everyday life, is that a thing truly is what one thinks it to be. If you think a rope is a snake, it is a snake; if you think brass to be gold, it is gold; if you think an idol to be the living and omnipotent God, it is such. This illustrates what has been said, and will again be said in succeeding lectures, that the weakness of the Hindu mind and character is largely a lack of all-around and sane development, a lack of proportion or balance. The East is weak where the West is strong. And in passing, that may now be suggested which will later be more fully dwelt upon, viz., that the West is weak where the East is strong. I suppose the sounder principle would be that, though a man must temporarily act on his immediate perception of things and for the present assume things to be what they appear, he should not continue to assert that things truly are only what they seem to be. Yet this unbalanced faith is almost the principal thing by which the Hindu is influenced in his religion. He does not wish to test his faith and by testing reassure himself that his assumptions are true. It is enough that his ancestors and he have always believed and acted as they have. Why should he even consider the desirability of changing? So, if God is everything and everywhere, as his sub-conscious pantheistic assumption implies, then if he believes that the idol is God, it is really so. In other words, while the Occidental sometimes overemphasizes the function of reason as essential in normal and sane mental processes, the Hindu, abnormally minimizes it.

Another mental characteristic of the Hindu mind, due to his powerful imagination, is that he is an idealist. He considers that the thing that ideally ought to be really is. The working of such idealism often perplexes Hindus in understanding Occidentals, and leads the former to charge the latter with untruthfulness. *E. g.*, if a Hindu comes to you and asks you to give him employment, you may reply, "I am sorry to say that I have no vacancy whatever." "But, if a vacancy should occur at some time, then would you give it to me?" "I have no idea that such a vacancy is likely to occur. Then why should I hold out any hope to you?" "Yes, of course, no vacancy may occur, but *if* one should occur, *then* would you not remember me?" "Well, I can make no definite promise whatever, but if a vacancy should occur, I should probably think of you, and *if* you then should seem the best man for the place, I should offer you the position." The man goes away and soon forgets almost all that you have said except the last clause, "I should offer you the position." Then much later if a vacancy should occur and you should not appoint the man to it, he would charge you with having broken your promise. The idealist does not give weight to conditions which stand in the way of what he desires. Those are like the small dust in the balance. What he remembers and expects from you is the fulfillment of his ideals. Why should he not expect from a great and good man like you whatever he wishes? One of the first and most important lessons for a missionary to India to bear in mind is to make no conditional promises whatever. His hearer will rarely remember or value the force of conditions in a promise. And if a promise, apart from its conditions, is not kept, the maker will probably be thought to have broken his promise.

Pantheism has dangerously weakened the moral as well as the mental working of the Hindu mind. Pantheism, and its accompanying doctrine of illusion which does away with the reality of intellectual distinctions, also logically and naturally does away with the reality of moral distinctions. The Hindu has a conscience because God speaks to his sense of right and wrong. But that conscience is weakened by unreal assumptions about God and reality. The Hindu does not consider that to be wrong which trained ethical sense considers wrong. But assuming the unreality of moral and mental action injures both conscience and mind. Also caste, which is the principal thing in modern Hinduism, has still more weakened the conscience. For right is not what is consistent with the nature of God or the universal ethical standard, and wrong is not what is inconsistent with the same. They are what custom and religion state them to be: they are inconsistency with arbitrary caste rules. Therefore not lying, nor breaking the seventh commandment, nor stealing is so heinous according to the code of caste as drinking a cup of water from the hand of a low-caste man, however clean that hand may be.

Another mental law which the foreign missionary to India at first is almost sure not to bear in mind, and which even the experienced missionary frequently disregards, is that words and ideas which have one meaning in the West, often have a very different meaning in India. God, sin, salvation, holiness in the Upanishads and in the code of caste really have a very different signification from the signification of those same words in Christian lands. It is sometimes said to a new missionary that he should not be surprised if the people of the country do not understand their own language. The suggestion implies the need of caution lest he use words which to his hearers will have a very different significance from that which those words have in his own mind. And he frequently makes serious mistakes in idiom, which result in his giving a very different meaning to his hearers from that which he intended. However, words in every language are constantly changing their meaning, and so after long contact with Christian teaching such words as God, sin, salvation, repentance, holiness are acquiring in the Indian vernaculars a new and Christian significance.

Another characteristic of the Hindu seems an anomaly, but is one which can be accounted for. Caste is probably the most ironclad institution that ever repressed the freedom of men's actions, and to some extent also their freedom of thinking. Yet it is often truthfully said that the Hindu mind is remarkably hospitable to new ways of thinking. The Hindu readily incorporated a considerable part of Buddhism into his own religion. The Hindu mind freely holds both pantheism and polytheism to be true. The Hindu is quite ready to admit Christ to his pantheon and to give Him almost the highest place, but without giving up any of his own inherited positions which are inconsistent with Christianity. The Hindu who has not come under the spell of the Western *Zeitgeist* has no hesitation in accepting every word of the Bible and every miracle recorded in it as true, and also the traditions and medieval miracles of the Roman Church, without at all giving up his own Hindu ideas. How does this come about? I think the explanation is twofold. It was said of the Germans long ago, that since France had dominion of the land through her armies, and Great Britain had dominion of the sea by her naval power, there was nothing left for Germany but the air, and so she sought dominion in thinking and philosophy. So when ritual and caste dominated with heavy hand the outward life of the Hindu, he sought and secured at least some measure of liberty, and took it in thought. For caste and the ritual of popular Hinduism do not care what the individual thinks or says, if only he does not openly disregard caste regulations. The recent contact with Western civilization is rapidly and powerfully weakening the ideas and practices of caste, so that now in many places Hindu religious leaders think it impolitic and useless to punish even open violation of caste. But probably even before this modern period disregard of caste was not punished, if this was not openly flaunted before the public. The genius of Hinduism would not express itself in a formative principle like that word of Christianity which says, "As a man thinketh in his heart, so is he." As a man acteth outwardly so is he, is the standard of caste. A second explanation of the omnivorousness of the Hindu mind is that pantheism has led Hindus to disallow or minimize distinctions. Therefore Hindus are ready to accept almost anything as true, and are not impressed by the logical consideration that both of two mutually contradictory positions cannot be true and helpful.

Understanding such characteristics of the Indian mind will explan why Hindus, when they become Christians, do not and cannot have the religious experience which people had in New England a generation ago when men were deeply agitated for personal sin and expressed repentance in pungent language and in prompt and expressive acts. When Hindus become Christians it is rarely from a strong sense of sin and of need of forgiveness. They have not inherited or developed sensitive consciences which call for relief from ethical wrongdoing. They become Christians principally because by the teachings and example of Christian leaders they are satisfied that the Christian way of living is the better way for time, and are assured that it is better also for the unknown future. They are drawn to become disciples of the Lord Jesus Christ by His character and teachings; *i. e.*, they feel *bhakti* or trustful love for Jesus Christ. They are drawn toward Him, and therefore become His disciples. According to the direction of Jesus Christ Himself it is not until the Holy Spirit takes of the things of Jesus Christ and applies these to the Indian adherents of Christ that He convicts them of sin for ethical shortcomings. This being so, the missionary should not wonder that marked repentance is not at first strong among Indian Christians. Such manifestations are not to be soon expected from that type of mind which the Hindu has inherited from generations of ancestors, and from social conditions which caste and polytheism have developed. These considerations also show how Hindus are likely to move in masses more than as individuals. Mass movements are likely to sweep considerable communities at a time into the Christian fold.

The case of one of the most interesting and eminent converts to Christianity in Western India illustrates how one type of the Hindu mind works. Like the early Hindu reformers he had become impressed with the social evils of his land. He saw that caste was splitting up the community into selfish and injurious relations, and he knew that India can never rise so long as it remains in the baneful bondage of caste. Also he knew that nothing but a religion would put away caste. So without any knowledge of Christianity, but no doubt under the inspiration of God, he began to study what religion India should have in place of Hinduism. At first, he naturally thought of Mohammedanism, about which every Hindu knows something. And he reasonably thought that Mohammedanism has some greater and more powerful truths than Hinduism in its emphasis on the truth of one personal and righteous God, in its doctrine of the harmfulness of idolatry and the need of spiritual worship, and especially in its theoretical teaching about the error of caste pride, and to some extent in its practical influence in abolishing caste distinctions. But as he thought still more he became convinced that Mohammedanism was not the religion which India needs, because it largely depends upon compulsion and not on reasonableness in enforcing its authority. So he began to think of developing an eclectic religion in which the best characteristics of various religions might be combined. This way of thinking is very much in accordance with the Hindu mind. While in this state of search, this man met a European in a railway train and talked with him about his intention. The European asked him if he had ever read the Bible or knew about Jesus Christ. The man said "No," but promised to read the Bible and find out about Christianity. Accordingly the European then and there gave him a New Testament; and largely without the personal influence of Christian teachers that capable and enterprising Hindu gentleman was so attracted by the Jesus Christ who is delineated in the Gospels, and so delighted with His way of leading men into spiritual life by spiritual means, that he soon became a Christian. He became a Christian, not from a personal sense of sin, but because he believed that Jesus Christ could help his country and save it from its injurious social condition.

Another instance will also show how the Hindu mind works. On one occasion at a meeting of the Bombay Missionary Conference I told how I was accustomed to preach Christ to Hindus. At the close of my remarks a Parsi convert, who has become an earnest Christian preacher, asked if I was accustomed, when preaching, to tell people that they were born in trespasses and sins. I replied, "Never." He said, "Is that taught in the Bible, and do you believe it?" I replied, "Yes, it is taught in the Bible, and I believe it." "Why do you not then preach it?" I said, "Because that is not part of the good message which I have to give to men. It is hard enough to make men realize that they are now in trespasses and sins for which they themselves are responsible, and to make them come to Christ in order to get away from trespasses and sins. If I should say that they were born in trespasses and sins, they would probably lay it on to their parents, and the more excuse themselves from responsibility." This led another missionary to say that a short time before Dr. Wilson, one of the most eminent Scotch missionaries in Bombay, had told him that when speaking to a Hindu about the burden of sin, that Hindu had told him that he himself seriously felt the burden of his own sins. It is so rare for a missionary to have any Hindu speak of being burdened for a sin of his own that Dr. Wilson asked the man with interest if he would tell him what those sins were of which he so felt the burden. The man instantly replied that they were his wife and mother-in-law. He felt as people in America very commonly feel, that there was a good deal of sin which was causing him much trouble, but it was the troublesome doings of others, not of himself, which were a burden to him. Principally it was the word "burden" and not the word "sin" in Dr. Wilson's remark which stuck in that Hindu's mind. He had a real burden because he was inconvenienced by things which his wife and mother-in-law had done. So when he spoke of carrying burdens connected with wrong-doing, the missionary supposed he was making a confession of unease due to his own sin. This story illustrates a common experience of Hindus. They are often ill at ease. They do feel burdened by many of the trying experiences of life and they desire relief from that unrest. They are uneasy because they are not in right relations to God, and it will be because Jesus Christ more than any other religious teacher brings into the Hindu mind and heart and conscience that revelation of God which makes the Hindus conscious of God's love and desire to help men that they will become Christians more than by any other influence.

The more we know of the Hindu mind, the

more it becomes clear that the Lord Jesus Christ is the One who is fitted to satisfy that type of mind. He satisfies the imagination of the Hindus. His teaching has that universal character which is in accordance with the hospitality of thought which characterizes the Hindu mind. He gives relief from the bondage of ritual and sacrifice and caste from which the heart and mind of the Hindu has long sought release, as the heart of man everywhere seeks relief. There is much criticism of Christendom in India, and rightly so, for how much of Christendom is not Christian! There is much hesitation in India to accept what is naturally considered Western theology. But there is no criticism of the Lord Jesus Christ. He meets and satisfies the Hindu intellect, the Hindu heart, the Hindu life, as no one else. And He is winning India to Himself. He will win it wholly. Keshab Chundar Sen well said, "It is Christ who rules British India, and not the British government. None but Christ, none but Christ, none but Christ, have deserved this bright, this precious diadem, and Jesus shall have it."

IV.

MISSIONS AND SOCIOLOGY

THE individual is the concrete expression of the associated life of man; and society is the associated life of individuals. Therefore sociology as the science of social phenomena is to-day, like psychology, a study of absorbing interest and vital importance. Religion being preëminently the doctrine and practice of men in relation to one another in their interpretation of God, sociology is a science of exceptional value to the religious teacher and leader. The history of religion in some broad sense is almost the history of sociology. What is the so-called Mosaic system but an attempt to regulate the relations of the men of Israel under a sense of responsibility to God? Thoughtful and experienced men in the West now value the historical and analytical study of social phenomena in showing how many past efforts to do good have been mistaken, and in pointing out the path to meet present problems.

The leaders of life in America now understand that wise charity can only be exercised when administered on those lines which sociology teaches to be sensible. It is well known that charity as formerly administered cannot cure one-tenth of the evils which it seeks to cure, while it often creates new evils in its well-meant, but mistaken, efforts to do good.

If the scientific study of social phenomena is important for the religious leader in his own land, how much more so is it for the man who, with little experience of work among his own people, goes to labor in a foreign land, among men of different climate, diverse race, history, customs, religion, and assumptions! This would seem almost axiomatic. Yet it has not been understood by missionary societies and by missionaries as it should have been. However, this is not strange, because scientific sociology is a comparatively recent study, even in the West. Nor is it surprising that even among primitive peoples, and still more among advanced peoples like the Japanese, Chinese, and Hindus, it is sometimes said of some missionaries, "Save us from our friends." It is likely to be said of those missionaries who think it easy and right to propose and push sweeping changes of custom, without understanding the basis of those customs in the light of the history of society in those lands. Yet it speaks much for the good sense of the average missionary that he has usually been prudent and far-sighted in the course which he has followed in seeking to modify and to mold social customs and institutions.

Of all countries probably India is the one which has the most complex social phenomena: where individualism is the least developed: where custom is most supreme. So that before all others the missionary to India should be one who has studied not only the history of society in his own land, but in other lands, and who goes to India anxious and ready to learn many things before trying to teach all things. Almost the worst thing which could happen to a young missionary going to any land would be to have the ability to use the vernacular immediately upon landing. With the best of intentions he would make many needless mistakes. There are "Training Homes for Missionaries" in America which think they are doing missionary candidates good service by teaching them in this country the vernaculars of India. This is almost sure to lead those candidates to form some bad mistakes in pronunciation and in idiom in the use of the languages so acquired. It also prevents the young missionary from going through that most important preliminary experience of getting gradually accustomed to the ideas and ways of the people before he ought to attempt much in teaching them. The chances are that missionaries from such training homes will begin and will long continue their work on the assumption that what they ought to do is to teach those people the imitation of Western ideas and customs. One of the chief temptations of the dogmatic type of young missionary is to marvel at the ways of experienced workers and to count them old fogies and behind the times. Fortunately most young missionaries are not of this type.

But the missionary—whether recent or long in the land—is sure to do some injury to himself and to his work and to the people, if he fails to realize the fundamental laws which have always controlled and which should control all social and religious progress. The first of these principles is the law of continuity. Just as in physical life the present is the outcome of the past, so in psychical life the present is the product of the past. He who would rightly judge of the present must bear in mind this law of continuity in psychical as in physical life. The past must be and will be modified. But what is wise and what is unwise in each case must depend considerably on what the past calls for. Customs and institutions are the skeleton of the social organism, and just as the skeleton of the human body must and should considerably determine the plans for the development of that body, so the skeleton of the past psychical body must and should largely determine plans for the development of the future psychical body. This is simply another way of saying that heredity as well as environment determines and should determine the constitution of the social organism, as it does the constitution of the physical organism. Therefore, it is important both to understand the heredity of the social constitution, and to bear it in mind when considering a new social environment for the future best development of any form of society.

This implies—what in missionary activity has not always been sufficiently understood, nor followed—that so much of good as is in the structure or in the possibilities of indigenous society in any land should be thoroughly understood and appreciated and utilized. In other words the missionary should follow the controlling principle of the Lord Jesus Christ, in social matters as well as in what are called purely religious matters, viz., the missionary should try to fulfill, and not to destroy. What did Jesus or the early apostles direct the early Christians to give up in their social organization, or in their religious organization? They did not give up the temple, or the synagogue, or any of their social habits. They did not cease observing Saturday as their Sabbath. They only added to the use of Saturday as Sabbath the recognition of the first day of the week as the Lord's day. And so not abruptly, but gradually, there came in the Christian community a transfer of the day of rest from the seventh to the first day of the week. At first both days were more or less observed. But at last without any upheaval the first day became the sole Sabbath of the Christians of the world.

It also has not been sufficiently understood that it is a mistake to assume that the social structure of any country should be changed from its own type into the American type. Changed it must be, and will be; infused with, and molded by Christian principles and motives it should be; and by God's grace it eventually will be changed into a Christian civilization. But it will be a different type of civilization from that which prevails in America. Change is not always improvement; or it may be only partial improvement and partial deterioration; and change in an undesirable and effete type of society may produce only partially desirable results. Under the influence of Christian missionaries some social changes in some lands have probably wrought more evil than good. But that is simply saying that good-intentioned people have made mistakes in other lands just as they have in America. In short, what may be good for the West, may not only not be *now* good for the East; it may be even undesirable now; though later the development of society there may approximate the type of society in the West. This in no way implies that Christian ideas and principles should not control everywhere. The world's way of living in society is bound eventually to be the way of the principles of the Lord Jesus Christ.

It is hazardous to generalize upon anything in India, because, as has been intimated in a previous lecture, the structure of society there, as the structure of religion, is not altogether homogeneous. India is not and never has been one nation. It is a conglomerate of races and of social phenomena. This is one reason why people who talk about that country differ so much in their statements and in their opinions. In the most backward classes there is still a comparatively primitive type of society. In other classes there is an advanced type of social organization. And yet it seems safe to say that, in general, society in India is more in the intermediate state. It certainly is the country where individualism is at the minimum and where social solidarity is most pronounced.

The missionary to India needs to remember

that the life of society has a physical basis. Man cannot wholly rise above his physical environment. The upward trend of society comes when environing forces are gradually modified. But sometimes the combination of those very forces with the working of some new forces enables men eventually to make those very forces which pressed them down become the means of rising higher. India's physical environment has largely developed its social structure. Its climate is on the whole enervating. Its soil is so rich that without strenuous toil it produces enough for the sustenance of the body. So Indians naturally have not been energetic. Shut out from much contact with other nations of the world by high mountains and by the sea, India has led a self-contained life. When successive torrents of invaders from the northwest poured through mountain passes to overwhelm the land the Indian easily submitted. This submission was mainly physical, and yet the conquest affected the internal structure of society.

The family organization of India involves many questions which the missionary should consider and understand. The type of family in

India is that of the united family where three generations live together. This has been partly due to economic considerations. There have been few moral restraints on the increase of numbers, and therefore it has been necessary so to organize the family as to minimize expenses and to multiply the means of support. Naturally this has been accomplished by having two and three generations united together and living in a common building. And this made it necessary for the women and even for the children to work for the support of the united family. This organization of the family largely controlled the position of women. It made the head of the united family very much the arbiter in settling all questions for the whole group. It compelled the younger women to be subject to the older women. It greatly limited education. It placed the discipline of most of the members of the family in the hands of one or two. In India, as in all tropical countries, sexual instincts are early developed and are strong. This has been one main reason for early marriages in that country. And so long as early marriages are the rule, the united family system has some advantages over the smaller and separate family system of the West. As this family system has affected the marriage system, and as in turn the marriage system has affected the family system, it ought to be evident to the Western missionary that none of these customs can be, or should be, hastily changed. Yet how hard it is for young missionaries from America, especially for unmarried young ladies, to appreciate that the marriage customs and family customs of India are not so harmful as they seem at first to people who have a different system, and that such marriage and family customs should not be radically changed at short notice. The missionary rightly seeks to give boys and girls an education in schools, and to give the brightest of them an advanced education. He easily supposes that education is mainly a matter of the study of books in schools. But the Indian united family system, with its early marriages, made an education for girls through books usually out of the question. A girl was betrothed, as we say, or, as the Hindus say, married, at an early age. In order to fit into the future united family life of her husband she has to spend a part of every year in the home of that husband even while she is a girl, in order to learn to take her part in that united family life. She spends only a part of her time in her own home. This interferes with study. Very early she becomes a mother and has to carry maternal responsibilities. Education for the boy has in India always implied more study of books than education for the girl. So in those families where such education was prized it was possible for the boy to go on with the study of books even when he had paternal responsibilities, because his own support and the support of his wife and children could be assured through the common means of the united family. This combined some advantages with some disadvantages. But when the missionary from the West sought to give to girls an education through books, and rightly realized the importance of postponing to a later date than Hindu custom allowed the entrance of those girls into the responsibilities of motherhood, the practical question would arise as to *how* long marriage should be postponed, and how long education through books should continue. How difficult it inevitably is for unmarried ladies who have been brought up in the advantages of life in the West and who have never studied the history of marriage and the history of society in non-Christian lands to realize the danger of postponing too long the marriage of girls whom they are training in schools. Perhaps it is impossible, and it certainly is most difficult, for such Western missionaries at first to realize the danger of immorality in thought, if not in deed, through greatly postponing the marriageable age of boys and girls in such lands. It requires not a little of the teaching of history and of experience as well as of idealism to decide upon the best age for this fundamental matter. Similarly in India all arrangements for marriage between young people are settled not by themselves, but by their elders. The wisdom of this course is one of the very hardest matters for young missionaries, especially for young ladies from America, to realize. But this custom has so many advantages that radical change in the matter of making matches should not be suddenly attempted. Happiness in the married state does not depend upon the way in which young people enter into it. It depends on whether the young man and the young woman are truly mated or not. If they are truly mated and fitted to be helpmeets of one another, they will live happily together however it came about that they were made man and wife. Whereas, though without the intervention of any other person they absolutely settle for themselves that they should become husband and wife, if they are not truly mated, their married life is apt to be anything but satisfactory. Yet in the West it is largely assumed that the only reasonable and satisfactory way for a male and female to decide whether to become husband and wife is for themselves entirely to settle the question after more or less courting and without much counsel from relatives and elders. But in India, where the parties are young, and where for many reasons it is not wise or feasible for the two sexes to have much intercourse, and so for boys and girls to be intimate or to know much about each other and each other's families, the prudent way for good matches is for the elders to take the initiative, and also to have a large part in deciding whether a marriage between a boy and a girl is a wise one or not. The two changes which Christian civilization ought soon to bring about and does bring about are, first: that the age of true marriage should be *somewhat* deferred; and second: that neither boys nor girls should be required to enter into the marriage relation without their own consent and without something of a desire for such a relation. Missionaries are bringing about these two changes as fast as practicable. But at first the young and inexperienced missionary thinks it very strange, and even improper, that he or she or relatives should be expected or allowed to have much part in making matches for Christian young people. "That is a matter which the young people must entirely settle for themselves without consulting me or anyone else," is the first impulse of the missionary from the West who has no knowledge of the history of marriage in India or experience of the mistakes which come when the missionary fails to use his or her influence in the matter. Nor is it alone in India, but in many another missionary land, that wise missionaries find it very desirable that they should have considerable part in helping the youth in their schools and the young men and women in the Christian community and the parents of young people in deciding wisely in the most important matter of selecting husbands and wives. In other directions also the marriage question is in some respects one of the most perplexing for the missionary. The principle of the Bible rightly assumes that a man should not marry a woman with whom he cannot have sympathy in religion, as in other matters, and so marriage with an unbeliever was strongly discountenanced by the apostle Paul. But he did not have in mind that state of society which exists in many missionary fields in India. It is not likely that the Christian man whom Paul had in mind would have had any difficulty in finding a Christian wife; or that he would be unable to meet his responsibilities, if he was unable to marry a Christian wife. But in some missionary fields in India the situation is very different. In all the early stages of missionary effort in India men become Christians in larger numbers than women, because the women are more secluded and have fewer opportunities for Christian instruction and inspiration. Moreover, as a Christian community grows the effort is made to give as many Christian girls as possible an advanced education. A well-educated girl ought to have, if possible, an educated husband. But it is by no means an uncommon occurrence that when the number of Christian men exceeds the number of Christian women it is impossible for some of those men to get a Christian wife. It is not desirable nor safe for many men to live in celibacy. In India a widower with a family of little children often cannot get a Christian woman to go into his home and be a mother to his children. Yet the Pauline injunction, "Be not unequally yoked with unbelievers," is supposed to be conclusive in settling that a Christian man can only marry a baptized woman. Under the stress of such circumstances it is not at all uncommon for a Christian man to marry an unbaptized female, even though he knows that this will result in his being excluded from church membership. The duty of that Christian widower to his children requires him to take another wife. He can get a non-Christian woman who is uninstructed in religious matters to become to him a faithful wife and to his children a good mother; but he cannot get a Christian wife. Ought the Pauline injunction to be stretched to cover that case?

Ought he to be disciplined if, though for years he has sought a Christian wife and cannot get one, he takes a non-Christian? To avoid this difficulty, some missionaries sometimes quickly baptize such a woman, in order that she may technically be called "Christian." But manifestly this is debasing the rite of Baptism, and of course it is regarding merely the letter, and not the spirit of the Pauline command. Or sometimes when a Christian man has for years sought in vain for a Christian wife the stress of circumstances leads him into illicit and sinful relations with a woman with whom he would have liked to contract honorable marriage, but was prevented by the Pauline injunction. Modern sociology shows that history cannot absolutely settle such questions. In accordance with modern views of God and the world it should be recognized that the apostolic command in question is not the sole authority for the settlement of questions very unlike those which called forth that injunction. Does not the principle which Jesus Christ applied to the Sabbath question apply also to the marriage question? Would not the Christian principle be that marriage is made for man, and not man for the marriage ideas of Biblical times?

Similarly the Christian missionary rightly considers caste an institution which in many respects is more opposed to the spirit of Christ than any other social institution of India. He therefore, in season and out of season, rightly seeks to break down its unbrotherly characteristics. But when the question comes of the wisdom of marriage between people who, though originally of different caste, have become Christian, it does not follow that because people of one social origin object to marrying people of another social origin, therefore they are wrongly influenced by caste. Nor does it follow that it is wise often to promote inter-marriage between people of different social origins. For a man marries not only his wife, but he enters into close social relations with all that wife's relatives. And a wife marries not only her husband, but enters into close social relations with all his relatives. So the practical situation makes most missionaries very slow to favor easy and promiscuous marriages between people of different social origins.

The question of polygamy is a social question not so easily settled in every state of missionary work as would be at first supposed by the people of America and by the inexperienced missionary. It was Sarah herself who gave to the father of the faithful her servant Hagar to wife. The unfortunate outcome of that action depended partly on the fact that Sarah herself later became the mother of a son. Had that not been the case, who can tell what the history of the Abrahamic family would have been? So in India, where even more urgent views are held as to the importance of the family line being continued than were held among the Hebrews, it is not uncommon that a Christian wife, who has no children herself, proposes to her husband that he should take a second wife. In my first year of missionary life a man once asked for admission to the Christian church who had two wives. He had taken the second wife because the first had no children. But later the first wife also became the mother of a son. When he applied for admission to the church he was told by the strong Indian Christian pastor that it was necessary for him to put away one of his wives. Neither wife wished to leave him. Neither wife was conscious of having done him or anyone any wrong. Each was the mother of a son, and each naturally asked "Why should I be put away from my husband and home?" But the rule of the church forbade the reception of a man with two wives. And he was encouraged to feel that it was more important that he should join the church than that he should retain both wives. So at last, contrary to her wish, he gave a writing to one of the wives, saying that she was free to go where she pleased and do as she pleased, and that so long as she remained otherwise unmarried and remained good, he would give her a small monthly alimony. Then he was received into the church. But the result was that that faithful wife who was put out of her home came to lead a bad life. With more experience I now very well see that the proper course to have been followed was to have said to the man, "We will not receive you into the church because you have two wives. But, because you have brought them into that relation, and have made them mothers of sons, you cannot rightly desert either or compel her to leave your care and support. Whenever in the course of events you may be the husband of only one wife, if you then live as a Christian man, and wish it, we shall receive you into our fellowship."

In the Jewish Church and in the early Christian Church it was not by radical and severe enactments that polygamy was put away. Like slavery it disappeared under the dynamic of Christian principles. So far as I know, most missionary societies in India would now naturally follow the course which I have indicated, viz., they would decline to receive a polygamist into church membership, but would not thereby deny that he might be a Christian at heart and a Christian in life.

The history of social institutions has instruction for the Christian missionary in the important matter of knowing how to deal with vice. It is claimed, I do not know with how much accuracy, that in some districts in England the institution of a good many homes for fallen women is increasing, instead of diminishing, immorality. Under the ordinary working of God's law sin is followed and should be followed by its natural evil consequences of all kinds. This is not inconsistent with the Christian principle that by God's grace men may give up their sin, and that some of the evil consequences of sin will be put away, and that there is no greater privilege and duty for the Christian than to be one who saves others from their sins, and helps the repentant sinner to escape from such consequences of the sin as he can escape from. Yet that does not imply that while men and women repent of sin they should be easily shielded from as many of the natural results of wrong-doing as possible. Sociology teaches that it is a complicated and difficult question to know how to deal with vice in the West. It is important for the missionary to know the teachings and principles of sociology as to the best ways of dealing with vice in non-Christian lands where the social institutions are different from those in the West. Yet I presume it would be a matter of great astonishment to most missionaries to hear that some good men and women in England have some doubts as to the entire wisdom of multiplying such institutions as have just been mentioned; and that therefore it does not certainly follow that such institutions should be multiplied in non-Christian lands.

Education is principally a social phenomenon. How much modern ideas of education have been changed in this land in recent years! How much scientific pedagogy is now required before even a college-bred man or woman is employed as an instructor in the public schools of some cities, and in private institutions! How much emphasis is now placed upon kindergarten, upon manual training, upon school discipline, upon cultivating the æsthetic taste! And similar pedagogical qualifications will soon be thought to be essential and will become common among missionary candidates. The last word on co-education may, or may not, have been said for America. In a land like India co-education is only beginning to be proposed and attempted, for the logical situation has legitimately led the missionary to be slow in proposing it in the schools. Yet probably there is going to be much more of co-education in foreign lands.

Industry and charity are important social phenomena. The missionary has to follow some policy in regard to these questions. Indiscriminate and unwise charity has been almost the worst scourge of India. How far the missionary in that country can radically depart from old customs is not easy to decide. But certainly the wise principle is to displace the need of misplaced charity and to develop the industrial capacity and habits of the land. On this principle nowadays the industrial side of missionary effort is rightly receiving and is likely to receive more attention.

The Indian missionary is sometimes charged with denationalizing Indian Christians. There is danger on this point. It is easy to increase a sense of need and dissatisfaction with economic ways and surroundings. So far as this dissatisfaction stimulates adequate exertion for the supply of those needs, so far the missionary does well. But in schools and churches to increase the needs and habits of people which their own resources cannot meet or supply is not true kindness. It is now realized that it is not a wise policy to take children, even famine children, far from their own district and surroundings, though in the new place they may get better care for body and mind. After they have had this care and are grown up, they may not be fitted to remain in their new habitat. In the long run it might have been better for them to have had fewer opportunities in their own district.

More distinctively religious questions also are in some measure sociological. The missionary who has been brought up with Puritan ideas about Sunday observance in the surroundings of New England life naturally imagines that keeping Sunday in the New England way is almost a *sine qua non*, if an Indian would be a Christian. But the social situation is so different there that it is impossible for many Christians to stop all Sunday work, just as unfortunately Sunday work is more common in New England now than it was years ago.

All government is a social relation, and so church government is essentially a sociological question. Men now see that history does not absolutely settle all questions of any kind. In new situations God's providence often gives new points of view. It is no longer believed by anyone in America that there is any divine right for kings. Any kind of government that secures the welfare of a people is ordained of God. Similarly it should now be seen that the Bible is not the sole source of authority in church government. What the Bible teaches and helps to secure is good order. Just as there are practically three types of secular government, all of which are divine: monarchical, aristocratic, and democratic, so there are three types of church government, all of which I believe to be historical in apostolic times, and all of which to have been of divine appointment. I believe that the right reading of the New Testament shows that in Palestine the first Christian Churches were Presbyterian in polity because they were Christian synagogues instead of Jewish synagogues, and the synagogue system is practically the Presbyterian system. In Greece the early churches were democratic or Congregational, for the very natural reason that the secular government was democratic; and since religion is not a separate compartment in which men think and act differently on Sunday from the way in which they think and act about all matters in the remaining six days of the week, the *ecclesiæ* of Greece were democratic in constitution and action, as the civil institutions of the land were. The monarchical principle prevailed in the Christian church in Rome. If this position is correct, the Bible shows that all three forms of church government are of apostolic and divine appointment. Similarly what form of church government shall now prevail in any land or any section of any land is settled partly by the heredity and partly by the surroundings of that church. Each form of government has its excellences and its weaknesses. That may be the better form of government for a community or a section of churches at one time than would be good at another period. Personally I am an episcopresbygationalist. That is, I try as a missionary to unite the excellences of the three types of church government. The circumstances of missionary responsibility compel me to be an *episco* or bishop, as every missionary in every land at first has been and must be. I settle a great many questions; I have a diocese in which I exercise large control. But in the churches of my diocese I develop *presbys*, *i. e.*, committees composed of leaders, as much as I can, because the leaders of a church in any community always have and must have exceptional fitness to exert an influence and therefore must and do lead. But I am also a *gationalist*. That is, I try in every church to help every member to feel a personal interest in all matters of the church, and by placing responsibility on him I try to qualify him to bear still further responsibility, and thereby to make him a more intelligent Christian, and a more effective member of the organization. My impression is that before we get through with it all types of church government in the West as well as in the East will be a good deal Episcopresbygational.

Whether a church should have a pastor or not; whether it should have only one pastor or not, is also a social question. The apostolic churches at first did not have pastors who gave their whole time to the service of the church in return for which those churches paid them salaries. In India most of the churches are not able to pay for pastors who give their whole time to the churches. As the community develops, it is more and more important that the leader in a Christian church should be a strong man with large capacity, and the need of some such pastors will be more appreciated. But the more difficult it will be for churches of limited resources to pay for such pastors. Because churches in the West should have pastors whose support they supply, it does not necessarily follow that this is the practical and best way for all missionary churches in every land.

Another very important sociological principle is how far a missionary should use authority, and how much he should depend upon personal influence apart from a claim to authority. Power to inflict penalties is one important element of authority. How far should a missionary be a man who can wisely inflict pecuniary penalties? How far should he rather let the Christian churches and community sometimes make mistakes and learn by experience to trust his judgment more, or how far should he depend on his own sense of what is right and good, in order to decide all social matters, even though the exercise of such authority should alienate and embitter the Christian community? Of course circumstances must help to decide all such questions. The situation may be different in one country or in one district from the situation elsewhere. One type of man can perhaps better follow one principle than another. But the missionary certainly needs to bear in mind one principle which he often easily forgets: viz., that the exercise of power of any kind is attended with serious dangers. What is the history of the priesthood in any land? Among the Hebrews, as among the Hindus, it teaches a most impressive and suggestive lesson: that the religious leader who uses authority of any kind may easily degenerate into a tyrant who comes wrongly to consider himself as an authority to settle the most important matters for those whom he ought to lead only by teaching and example. The power of the purse is a distinct danger to the modern missionary. The missionary can easily think that he or she should absolutely decide when a boy or girl should or should not come to school or leave school; or be married or not be married; or do this or do that, because the missionary has spent some money for that boy or girl. For past or future pecuniary favors which are in his hand he can come to think that even the parents or relatives of those children have lost their right or their qualifications to have much voice in settling such questions. In every single case where the people have had intelligence the history of modern missions has given a melancholy illustration of hard feeling, bitterness, estrangement, and even separation from the church and Christian principles when missionaries have seemed to be or really were arbitrary in thinking that they should settle all questions, though they might have retained the confidence of those whom they had alienated, had they been content to depend on influence rather than on authority. The Holy Spirit utters no commands: He influences men. The missionary should avoid the mistake of being limp; he should be decided in exercising proper discipline and in carrying proper responsibility for the use of money. Yet even when he disagrees with the Christians of his community he should remember that the greatest service he can render is to be a "holy spirit" himself, who by example and precept, in love and in gentleness, as well as by plainness of reproof, seeks to lead, rather than to drive those whom God in His mercy has brought into His fold.

V

A COMPARISON OF CHRISTIANITY AND HINDUISM*

THE scientific and thorough examination of the religions with which Christianity has come into contact is a recent undertaking, but a general comparison for practical purposes has been one principal part of missionary activity from the first Christian century. Paul did something of it at Lystra, on Mars Hill, and in his writings, especially in the first chapter of the Epistle to the Romans. At first the comparison of religions for practical purposes naturally dwelt on the unsatisfactory elements of non-Christian faiths. Formerly the offices of medicine largely sought to cure disease by fixing attention on abnormal conditions and on removing these by aid from without. There was little thought of internal, curative forces. So it was not unnatural that the offices of spiritual medicine were worked on the same assumption and method. From the very first the Chris-

* In preparing this chapter use has been made of Slater's *The Higher Hinduism in Relation to Christianity.*

tian missionary saw the weaknesses and unsatisfactoriness of non-Christian religions, and, believing that Jesus Christ was the only one to free men from those weaknesses, the missionary saw little good in those ethnic faiths. History has given much justification to that early method, for all the religions with which Christianity formerly came into contact, Greek, Roman, Scandinavian, Teutonic, Keltic, have passed away. No religion can die until it is supplanted by a better one, for man is essentially religious and must have some religion. The old religions passed away because they were not meeting the needs of men so well as they should: and since the Christian religion took their place, it is plain that the Christian religion was better than those which it supplanted. For nineteen centuries the verdict of experience has uniformly been that when any fairly pure type of Christianity has, for any considerable period of time, come into contact with other faiths, it has displaced them, and they have gone. When Islam came into contact with a corrupt type of Christianity in some parts of Europe, Asia, and Africa, it supplanted them, but it is not doubtful that it was a corrupt type of Christianity that went to the wall. In his "Rise and Influence of Rationalism in Europe" Mr. Lecky has said, "There is but one example of religion which is not necessarily subverted by civilization, and that example is Christianity." Even with this inspiring record of history as to the comparative value of Christian and non-Christian faiths, some Christians have objected to examining Christianity with other religions, as if the former had some special divine basis, which puts it in another class from other religions, and which should exempt it from scientific comparison. But the modern view of God and the world forbids such classification, and Christianity appears more certainly fitted to be the religion of mankind as it receives no different treatment than other faiths when all are compared with one another.

When comparing Christianity with other religions missionary advocates have sometimes unfairly compared the ideals of Christianity or the best phases of Christendom with the worst aspects of non-Christian religions. Of course this is not right. Yet it is not surprising, because human nature leads men for practical purposes to set roseate ideals against a strong delineation of evil conditions. Advertisements of all kinds illustrate this tendency of human nature. Often without intending to exaggerate, the characteristic advertisement would seem to imply that man could hardly find life worth living without the article recommended. It may be largely due to the same natural propensity that non-Christian advocates contrast the best ideals of their own sacred books with the current evils of Christendom, forgetting or ignoring the clear fact that most of those evils are due, not to the following of Christian principles, but to a disregard of those principles. Even in America, not a few intelligent people are strongly carried away by unfair and entirely misleading representations of the better phases of ethnic religions, and imagine that the fruits of the ethnic faiths correspond to the idealistic statements which are quoted. First-hand knowledge of the actual and legitimate fruits of those faiths would immensely surprise such people and cause a revulsion of opinion. Some people who call themselves Christians are nowadays often inclined to suppose that one religion is as good as another. Dr. John Henry Barrows, the President of the first Parliament of Religions at the Chicago World's Fair in 1893, was most anxious that a second similar Parliament of Religions should be held at Benares in order that the representatives of all other faiths might not only hear what can be said in praise of Hinduism, but might see its results in the most sacred city of that faith. But no shrewd Hindu would ever consent to issuing an invitation for such a Parliament to meet at Benares. In India the most expressive term for a cheat is "a Benares man." The one truth-seeking course is to compare the ideals of one religion with the ideals of other religions, and also the power of one and the power of the others to inspire both individuals and society measurably to realize their ideals. In other words, like phases of various religions should be compared. Any honorable student of comparative religion now seeks to follow this principle. Christian advocates certainly should be scrupulously desirous of treating all ethnic faiths with both justice and courtesy. Whatever may be the result to Christianity of a comparison of it with other religions, there is no doubt that the result of such recent comparison has been one cause of the modern view of God and the world, and that it certainly has increased reverence for God by increasing recognition of His continuous effort to reveal Himself to His human children. Such scientific and historic study of religions in all lands has given a new illumination to the words of the Lord Jesus Christ, "My Father worketh even until now, and I work." Nor has comparative religion yet led men to find reason for thinking that any other previous religion can take the place of Christianity hereafter.

With these preliminary remarks on the principles which should control the comparison of religions, I turn to some comparison of Christianity and Hinduism, because my experience is principally connected with the contact of these two faiths. In these lectures by religion I mean any people's interpretation in thought and in act of what God is trying to teach them by every revelation of Himself. As Hinduism means the heterogeneous ideas and practices which historically have been current in different types of Hindus, so Christianity means the varying ideas and practices which those who call themselves Christians have followed in their interpretation of God and of the world. The purest type of Christianity would begin with Christ and with the best interpretations of Him. But many types of Christianity have not been pure, and since Christianity is a growing religion, even up till now it has not become all that it is to be. In seeking to compare Hinduism and Christianity one should rightly compare only their similar aspects. However, since neither has had one consistent type and development, it is difficult to decide what are aspects which can be fairly compared. Not only do Greek, Roman Catholic, and Protestant types of Christianity differ in their interpretation of what is Christian thought and practice, but different schools in those different churches differ quite considerably among themselves. Nevertheless, there are large outstanding characteristics of religion as understood and practiced by most Hindus and by most Christians which can be fairly placed in comparison.

In general, it may be said that Hinduism starts from nature and interprets God through it, while by its fundamental and characteristic doctrine of incarnation in the Lord Jesus Christ Christianity starts with human nature, and in particular with the man Christ Jesus, and through Him and through less perfect humanity interprets God. This contrast is great and suggestive. Starting from nature rather than man, and always following that direction, how is it possible to arrive at a personal and at a high ethical conception of God? Though hero-worship, and respect for virtues, and reverence for Buddha entered into Hinduism as formative principles, they were entangled in earlier and lower elements. But the influence of even these somewhat human elements was again eclipsed by Vedantic pantheism, which unquestionably is the controlling element in advanced Hinduism, and is sub-conscious even in polytheists and idolaters. If any intelligent Hindu were asked for one phrase which is indubitably and universally Hindu, he would say it is "*ekam eva advitiyam,*" *i. e.*, there is only one It; no second. Dr. Deussen is the principal authority on Hindu philosophy. In his "Essay on the Philosophy of the Vedanta," he says, "The Vedanta is now, as in ancient times, living in the mind and heart of every thoughtful Hindu. It is true that even here in the sanctuary of Vedantic metaphysics, realistic tendencies, natural to man, have penetrated, producing the misinterpreting variations of Sankara's Advaita [pure pantheism]; . . . but India till now has not been seduced by other voices."

The character of any religion mainly depends on its conception of God. So we begin with the doctrine of God in Hinduism and Christianity. The Hindu pantheism has been the controlling element in forming the idea of God. Therefore the Hindu doctrine of God cannot be personal, and, if impersonal, it cannot be ethical. Even when some theistic doctrine appears in high phases of Hinduism as developed by Mādhvā and Rāmanuja, while it makes Brahma a personal, omnipotent, and omniscient God, it is very different from the Christian conception of God, because the former regards God as essentially different from the human soul. It seems fair to say that the highest Hindu conception of God as personal makes Him to consist of pure thought, without activity. The gods of the polytheists, and especially the gods of the modern Epics and Purānas, *i. e.*, the gods of popular Hinduism, have characteristics which are not models for good men to follow, and sometimes they are positively immoral according to the common understanding of the masses, though doubtless some of these interpretations degenerated from earlier and better meanings.

The doctrine of God even in the least ethical and least spiritual types of Christianity has been, and is, that He is a personal, ethical Creator and Ruler of the universe and that He is ceaselessly active. Theologies vary as to His dealings with sin and sinners, and have sometimes been such as are repellent to modern conceptions of right. But even those repellent theories were because men thought of God as just, and therefore compelled to safeguard His justice, albeit those theories made His efforts inconsistent with our present views of right. But the doctrine of God which naturally follows from the Christian doctrine of incarnation, is that God is like Jesus Christ, full of truth and grace. Who questions that this is the highest doctrine of God which men have held? Hinduism and Christianity have both a doctrine of incarnation which at bottom implies that when men are in trouble God is sure to come near to help them. But the Hindu doctrine of incarnation differs very much from the Christian doctrine. Of the ten incarnations of Vishnu the earlier ones are incarnations of God in animals, such as a fish, a tortoise, and a boar. Then comes a semi-animal incarnation as a man-lion, and later incarnations in human beings, though these human beings are in some respects unlike ordinary men.

Also in comparing the doctrine of man in Hinduism and Christianity we find a marked contrast. According to Christianity man is made in God's image and is God's child. According to the pantheistic school of Hinduism, which is always coupled with the doctrines of illusion and transmigration, man is not what he seems to be. He is one link in an indefinite chain of events. He once may have been an animal. In the next state of existence he may become another animal. Caste, which is the controlling element of popular Hinduism, has no dignity for man as man. For however good and capable a low-caste man may be, he can never in the present state of existence rise to the dignity of a man of high origin, however incapable and unethical that man may be, provided the latter does not violate the laws of caste.

The doctrine of God and of man involves the doctrine of sin. According to pantheistic Hinduism sin is mainly ignorance and yet partly the working of wrong acts in a previous state, and therefore it is mainly fate. Where the conscience of man asserts itself, sin is sometimes ethical wrong-doing, for which a man himself is responsible. Yet the word sin in its most common and most characteristic meaning expresses not doing that which is inherently and always wrong, but in particular it is disregard of caste requirements; it is an unfortunate condition, due as much perhaps to the action of others as to one's own responsible deeds. Being touched by a low-caste man brings a man into more difficulty, for which expiation must be made, than anger or pride. Among Christians also there have been low conceptions of sin. It has sometimes been understood to be disregard of commandments by the church, or by the priest. Yet probably there has been even in the lower types of thinking among Christians an ethical element, and certainly on the whole in Christianity sin is wrong-doing toward God and toward men and toward one's self, for which one is responsible and which results in making a man's soul unclean.

The doctrine of sin has as its counterpart the doctrine of salvation. Undoubtedly among Christian churches there have been, and still are, inadequate and even wrong conceptions of what salvation truly is. Even when salvation was largely thought of as a future condition in a safe place, there was some element of appreciation that it was a matter of character. Certainly in pure Christianity as taught by the Lord Jesus Christ salvation is simply and only soundness of character. Negatively it is salvation from sinning, and positively it is strength and virtue in the soul. In Hindu pantheism salvation is release from conscious existence. In caste it is remaining within the pale of caste requirements. In popular Hinduism it is getting favors of any kind from the gods.

In regard to the means of salvation there are points of contact and of contrast between Hinduism and Christianity. According to pantheism the principal means of securing bliss is by the path of knowledge. According to ordinary Hinduism it is through austerities and through the merit of many good works that sin can be atoned for and the person brought into a right condition. However, in Hinduism there is also a doctrine of grace according to which by the favor of the gods a sinner can lose some of the results of his wrong-doing and unfortunate condition. The word *prāyaschit*, meaning expiation or atonement, is a word of great significance and of common usage among Hindus. While it doubtless implies that a man who is in trouble recognizes that he has done wrong, and that he must make some expiation for wrong-doing, yet for the most part repentance is not thought of as any necessary part of such expiation. In modern times the word *prāyaschit* principally expresses the penance which a man must perform to do away with the results of disregard of caste regulations. For example, if an intelligent Hindu gentleman crosses the ocean in order to go to a foreign land for a higher education, even with the intention of thereby qualifying himself to serve his country better, he must on returning to India do penance, *i. e.*, make a *prāyaschit*, before he can be restored to society. Among some of the adherents of Christianity there have been mechanical conceptions of atonement. But in general even in the grosser types of the doctrine there was some recognition of the fact of suffering on God's part due to the sin of His human children, and of His hatred of wrongdoing as the essential element in the means of salvation which Christ revealed. And nowadays I suppose the understanding to be very common that the suffering of Christ expresses God's eternal sorrow for sin, and the profound truth that He must always suffer, when for any reason His human children fail to live up to right relations with Himself, and that the sufferings of Christ as expressing the sorrow of God are the way by which sinners are brought into reconciliation with their Heavenly Father, because through the sufferings of Christ as a revelation of God's suffering there awakens in the sinner's heart a sense of his own wrong-doing, and a repentance and a desire to sin no more. The doctrine of the Cross is central in Christianity as expressing God's eternal and infinite pain for sin in man and His readiness to do all that He can to reclaim them. In Hinduism there is no such doctrine whatever. In Christianity there is also prominent the fact that God's particular way of reclaiming men from weakness and wrong-doing and of drawing them into higher and purer life is by fellowship and example. Jesus Christ is a Saviour of men because He is Himself a man and is to us an elder Brother, who by His example, and by His fellowship with men, and by His suffering for men draws them to God. In Hinduism there is no Saviour. The highest way of salvation is the way of knowledge, which is a long and hard way which very, very few can even hope of traversing. For the common Hindu the main way of salvation is the way of works. But however much he may work, this is not supposed to bring him purity of character, though it may save him some steps in the long, long chain of transmigration.

One of the principal characteristics of Hinduism, and one about which much is now spoken in the West, is the doctrine of *karma.* The word *karma* really means *deed.* And the doctrine means that men must suffer the results of their deeds. This doctrine includes a large measure of important truth. It is akin to the common teaching of the Bible, "Whatsoever a man soweth, that shall he also reap." And the helpful truth in this doctrine is that retribution is not arbitrary: it is the exact, inevitable result of what a man has been and has done. But the practical weakness of Hinduism is that this doctrine is held alone, without the complementary and equally true doctrine that a man can escape in some measure from some of the results of wrong-doing, and also that he may lose by future wrong-doing some of the good which would result from past good deeds. It is the plain teaching of daily experience that men can forgive one another and can put away some of the results of their own wrong-doing and of the wrong-doing of others, and the supreme teaching of Christ is that God is trying to overcome *karma*, so that where sin abounded grace doth much more abound, and so the worst of sinners can have hope that by the help of the living God the trend of his past life and deeds can be changed and he can become a new creature. This latter is a doctrine which Hinduism does not know and cannot teach.

God has made men in India, as in other lands, know that truth and kindness and gentleness and patience and those principles which we in the West know as virtuous are desirable and helpful. His Hindu children have not been ignorant of these fundamental teachings of their Heavenly Father. Yet the Hindu religion has not emphasized such matters, and has often greatly obscured them. Where the way of knowledge is supposed to be the highest way of religion, and knowing all things to be illusory is the highest knowledge, or where meritorious deeds can purchase release from undesirable conditions, how can repentance and humility and gratitude and hope be naturally stimulated? The power of the doctrine of the Cross as developed by Paul finds its principal commendation in the fact that therein there is a power to produce sorrow for one's own sin, and humility for one's own weaknesses, and trust in God as the giver of grace, and gratitude for the receipt of undeserved kindness. These are the virtues which the Cross is fitted to develop in man, and it has developed them as no doctrine of Hinduism has any fitness to do.

According to the higher aspects of Hinduism there is no place for prayer. With an impersonal God and the working of an inevitable Fate in mind, how can any man pray? Yet prayer is instinctive in the human heart. Men in difficulty and in sorrow must more or less long for relief. So polytheism has in some measure provided a way for that which pantheism and karma cannot provide. Not prayers, but vows, are a considerable part of popular Hinduism. But vows are transactions whereby men seek to purchase some of the things which they desire. Whereas in Christianity prayer has a very high place. God being a living God and in ceaseless relations with all men, and especially being like Jesus Christ, prayer is one of the highest and most natural and most hopeful activities of the human soul. And Jesus Christ has not simply by His precepts encouraged men to pray, but by His example He has made men believe that the heart of God longs to respond to the upward look and appeal of His human children.

Sacrifice is always an element in religion. Among the early Hindus the sacrifice of animals was very prominent. There was a sacrifice of the horse, of the cow, of lesser animals, and sometimes even of man. But in the upward trend God was more and more showing men that the sacrifice of animals was not what he desires from His human children. Probably when Ashoka, the first great Buddhist monarch, was on the throne in the middle of the third century before Christ, he gave a great blow to sacrifice. The Buddhist and Jain doctrine of non-injury must have had great influence in deterring men from killing animals for religious purposes, and Ashoka's inscriptions in various parts of India show that he sought to prohibit that practice. Also philosophers in their doctrine of salvation by knowledge must have led men to see that sacrifice has in itself no real value. Similarly in Christendom after Christ the sacrificing of animals gradually died out. But a new idea of sacrifice, as the giving by God for men of His beloved Son and His continual suffering for them, brought into Christianity a higher conception of sacrifice. Under the inspiration of that divine example the sacrifices of Christianity, are those which love makes to enable God or to enable human beings whom men love to secure those objects which are dear to Him and to them.

In Western India even twenty-five years ago it was a common thing for most Hindus to say to the Christian missionary, "Your religion and ours are very different." Now, after contact with Christianity, it is far more common to say, "There is not much difference between your religion and ours." This great change illustrates what the result on Hinduism is of its contact with Christian teachings. Christian ideas and principles are gradually fulfilling and supplanting Hinduism. Yet there is another movement somewhat in the opposite direction, viz., a movement for the revival of Hinduism. But this is not strange, because religion is the nearest and dearest object to men, especially to conservative men.

One of the points in which Hinduism and Christian thought come nearest in words, though not so near in reality, is the desire for knowing the truth and in the conviction that it is possible to know the truth. The best minds of India have for many ages been eager and patient and self-sacrificing seekers for the eternal and the supreme. But to the Vedantist to know is to know metaphysically, to accept speculatively. And according to Hindu thought all that one can know is to deny that anything can strictly be predicated of the Supreme. It is without qualities (*nirguna*), without differentiations (*nirviseshika*), without limitations (*nirupadhika*). It is pure being, or pure thought, knowable "only by the withdrawal of the senses from every external object, of the mental faculties from their truest cognitions, and by complete suppression of the passions." Nothing can be affirmed of It because It is in no relation to us. Even the universal forms of thought are unreal. Whereas to the Christian knowing the Supreme is a true apprehension of a real, personal God, who is known not simply by the intellect, but also by the heart and by the will, just as we get acquainted with human beings. Christ's teaching is this: "This is life eternal, that they might know Thee, the only true God."

It is also a characteristic of both higher Hinduism and of Christianity that the only worthy object of knowledge is something spiritual, not material. Thus the Śvetaśvatara Upanishad VI. 20, says:*

> "When men shall roll up space,
> As it were a piece of leather,
> [that is, when the impossible shall happen]
> Then will come an end of evil
> Apart from knowing God."

And the Muṇḍaka Upanishad I. 2. 10, 11, says:

> "Thinking sacrifice and meritorious deed the chiefest,
> Naught better do they know,—deluded!
> Having experienced enjoyment in the vault of heaven won by good works,
> They re-enter this world or a worse.
>
> They who practice austerities and faith,
> Who dwell serene, possessing knowledge,
> They, being freed from stain, depart hence
> To where is the immortal Person, e'en the imperishable Spirit [Atman]."

* This and following quotations from the Upanishads are from a forthcoming *Translation of the Principal Upanishads,* by R. E. Hume, Ph. D.

In words, and in some true degree in reality, this thought resembles the teaching of Christ, who says, "Lay not up for yourself treasures upon earth, where moth and rust doth corrupt, and where thieves break through and steal: But lay up treasures for yourselves in Heaven." "Blessed are the pure in heart, for they shall see God." But the Christian sense of true knowledge is something different from metaphysical speculation, and is expressed in the words, "The world, in its wisdom, knew not God." So that there is a deep contrast between Hinduism and Christian thought about what constitutes the knowledge of the Supreme. The former is speculative knowledge: the latter is personal intimacy gained by all the powers of man. The speculative knowledge of the Vedantist results in his assuming that It is all, and that I myself am It. The practical knowledge of the Christian is that God is the Father of our spirits; that He is love; and that we have fellowship with Him as sons, similar to the fellowship which man has with man. Through knowledge to loss of conscious existence is the Hindu ideal: through the life of Christ, and later through our own purified life, to intimacy with the living God, is the Christian ideal. Thus, first on the testimony of Christ, as one whose own life gives assurance that He knows that whereof He speaks, and then by our own experience, we know God by our whole being, our intellect, heart, and will, and grow into intimacy with Him.

There is a contrast between the conception of the soul in the East and in the West. In the West the assumption is that the soul of man is a self-conscious intelligence and will. In Hinduism there is more than one conception of the soul. In the lowest types of Hinduism there is no clear understanding of the soul, but probably it is something which controls the body, without much thought of its nature or its future. In higher Hinduism the soul is practically a very rarified or etherealized body. According to the main belief of Hinduism, especially of the Sānkhyan philosophy, the universe is made up of innumerable souls and bodies. Every kind of body—mineral, vegetable, animal, human, and even divine—is possessed by a soul. At a particular time a particular soul occupies a particular body for some important reason. According to Hinduism the individual soul has three bodies. According to the Christian it has two. It has in this present world a physical body, the *sōma sarkikon* of St. Paul. And when the spirit leaves this physical body, it takes on a psychical body, the *sōma pneumatikon* of St. Paul. The Hindu says that the individual soul has, (1) a corporeal body (*sthūla śarira*); (2) it has a subtle, or psychic body (*sūkshma śarīra*), as minute as a point, composed of sense, volition, and cognition, which is built by his thoughts, and which accompanies the soul in all its migrations. In regard to these two bodies the Hindu idea approaches Christian thought. But, (3), he adds a third or causal body, (*kārana śarira*), which is not a real body, but is like a dreamless sleep, into which illusion will bring the soul. So both physical and psychic bodies are eventually to pass into this unreal body when consciousness shall cease.

What the future of the soul is to be after it leaves the body is not consistently taught in all types of Hinduism. Even the Bhagavada Gita, which is esteemed the greatest of the sacred writings of India, teaches that being virtuous is not the end of life, and that virtue does not bring the highest reward. Thus in IX. 20, 21, Krishna is represented as saying:

"Of me the knowers of the three Vedas, the soma-drinkers, the purified from sin,
When they sacrifice with offerings, request the way to heaven.
Reaching that holy, God-Indra's world,
They eat in heaven the heavenly feasts of the gods.

"But after having enjoyed that spacious heavenly world,
When their merit is exhausted they return to this mortal world.
Thus, though having followed the injunctions of the threefold [Vedas],
They who only desire desires obtain the transitory."

Similarly, the Brihad Aranyaka Upanishad IV. 3. 7 ff. teaches that purification from sin and the practice of virtues merits only a transitory reward; that this reward is enjoyed in a festive, sensuous paradise and that the heavenly climate has the effect of sapping and withering the little merit acquired, and when this is worn out its possessor comes back to this mortal, sinful world to begin the round again. But in the higher Vedantic system the loss of conscious existence in the supreme It is the *summum bonum* of the individual soul. According to the Brihad Aranyaka Upanishad II. 4, 12, "after death there is no consciousness." In the Chāndogya Upanishad VIII. 11, the father of creation, Prajāpati, teaches that the highest attainable condition of anyone is like profound, dreamless, unconscious slumber. According to the Māndukya Upanishad 7, the acme of existence for a person is the condition beyond profound slumber, "having no inner consciousness, nor outer consciousness, nor consciousness of either sort, not pure intelligence, nor intelligence, nor non-intelligence."

The doctrine of transmigration is one of the two principal doctrines of the higher Hinduism. In the early phases of Hinduism what might happen in another existence was not a common part of the fear which troubled men. Nor did the early Aryan settlers have any such doctrine as transmigration. But when the Hindus began to speculate on the problem of evil and on ultimate realities, they developed the most thoroughgoing doctrine of metempsychosis. In many systems of thought in the Orient, as well as in

Hinduism, matter is evil. Contact of the soul with matter causes impurity which must be removed. It can be removed by successive rebirths in all manner of bodies. Men whose conduct has been evil are to have as punishment rebirth in lower animals, even in vegetables and minerals. This doctrine has as its basis the pantheistic conception of the supreme. A metaphysical supreme It logically carries with it a metaphysical conception of man as not strictly personal, with no personal responsibility and with the desirability of eventually losing the untrue sense of personality which he now has. In the West, where the assumption is that, like the supreme soul, the individual soul of man is self-conscious intelligence and will, this doctrine of reincarnation and transmigration cannot be accepted, because a self-conscious intelligence cannot be suddenly transferred from one type to another most unlike type of existence such as that a man should become a mineral or vegetable or even animal. Yet the underlying truth of transmigration, though badly mixed up with metaphysical and ethical error, is a conviction of the continued existence of the soul after this present life. However, the working of the theory is considerably materialistic, because the merit or demerit of the soul in one state of existence mainly depends upon the particular body which it inhabits at the particular time. Again, this doctrine assumes the important truth that wrong-doing of any kind is necessarily followed by evil consequences, and this meets that sense of justice which is in every human heart. This doctrine has its attractiveness as an attempt to account for the mixture of good and evil in the world and for the inequalities of conditions and birth. Without a personal soul and without a personal and merciful God who is doing His best to develop into ethical union with Himself the souls he has made in His image, the transmigration doctrine is not an untenable one. It illustrates what has been emphasized in previous lectures, that it is simply an imperfect interpretation by the Hindus of that which God has been trying to teach and which the Christian interpretation states in a sounder way. What is lacking in the Hindu doctrine is better explained by the Christian teaching. Happiness and misery do not mainly depend on outward conditions: they depend on moral qualities. At heart the world knows by experience that the main differences between men are the conditions in the men themselves and not in their circumstances. Also, that even the conditions of every individual in this life depend very much on contact with other men and do not need an explanation from assuming a former state of existence. Modern thought still more confirms the Christian doctrine by throwing light on the two great forces of heredity and environment, although men have always known something of their power. Heredity and environment explain many of the perplexities which led the Hindus to the theory that conditions in this life are wholly due to actions in a previous state of existence.

No well-informed man now questions that heredity is one of the principal forces which work in forming and controlling men. The continuity and solidarity of the race are undeniable facts which are becoming more and more clear, and heredity works for both degeneration and regeneration. By it the individual receives from his ancestors for many generations his chief physical and spiritual characteristics and tendencies. Heredity works both retribution and beneficence. And the knowledge of this eternal law is more and more one of the principal forces to create a high sense of responsibility in mankind and to help it upward. Similarly, modern science shows how environment largely accounts for the condition and development of the individual. While a bad environment tends to reproduce crime, yet unquestionably on the whole the environment of men is more wholesome than unwholesome, and human nature responds to what God is doing for it through the manifold relations of society. These two laws, whose universal workings are indubitably demonstrated, show the reasonableness of the Christian doctrine of man as having his first existence in *this* world, and from this passing into the next world. Moreover, the Christian doctrine adds one supreme explanation to the enigma of life which the Hindu only vaguely understands, viz., that suffering has a spiritual value. Despite its perplexity, suffering is a part of God's wise and loving order in training men. This is in the plainest way confirmed by the life and work of Jesus Christ. He knew no sin, yet He was the greatest sufferer. But amid all His sufferings He was calm and hopeful because He understood the inevitableness and the function of suffering in a sinful world as expressing the necessary and eternal sorrow of God for the sins of men. It is the sorrow of God for the sins of His children which draws them into repentant, humble, and grateful relation to Him as sons. "Though Jesus was a son, yet learned He obedience by the things which He suffered; and has been thereby made perfect. And thereby having been made perfect He became unto all them that obey Him the author of eternal salvation." Heredity shows that men suffer on account of sin. Even God suffers on account of sin, and both His suffering and men's suffering is a means by which to overcome and banish sin.

The doctrine of transmigration is inconsistent with the doctrine of mercy. Transmigration is a system of impersonal, inexorable law. But some phases of Hinduism which formulate a doctrine of mercy show that transmigration does not meet the needs of the human heart which shows mercy to fellowmen and which cannot avoid the belief that the power who rules men will also show them mercy. Only so low is the sense of sin and so strange is the mercy, that even taking the name of God and bathing in sacred streams will wash away all sins according to the teachings of some types of Hinduism. Again, transmigration is opposed to the law of development which modern thought posits as universal. Transmigration teaches that for some demerit in some birth a man may have to go back and become a mineral, or a vegetable, or an animal. Modern thought teaches the continuity of the existence of every soul. Transmigration assumes the same, but it fails in the very point where it could unquestionably establish itself, if it were true, viz., in experience; because the individual soul which may have been through a thousand states of existence before it came into its present body in this world remembers nothing in its previous states of existence, as it should have done. So that the doctrine of transmigration is a mere assumption, and an unphilosophical one at that. Moreover, while seeking to satisfy the claim of justice in accounting for inequalities and evil in this world as a consequence of wrong-doing in a previous life, it is most unjust, for it claims to make men suffer for wrong which they do not know and cannot know that they have done. The human heart necessarily revolts against punishing anyone for assumed wrong which he does not know and cannot know that he has done. And still worse is it that transmigration is in no way remedial. It does no good to the sinning soul. It cannot show him what wrong he has done nor how that wrong has worked evil, and so it cannot make him penitent; and even after making him suffer in this world it perhaps sends him back to the impure surroundings in which he became impure, perhaps to dwell in a stone, or a pig, or a crow. It is a moral injury to men to make them believe that there can be sin with no possibility of consciousness of sinning, and to impress fatalism upon them, as the doctrine of transmigration does. According to that creed the results of unknown deeds are inevitable, while a man has neither ability to do differently nor consolation amid bereavement and trials for which he knows that he is not personally responsible. So transmigration offers no hope for this world or for the next. One illustration of the cruel form of the doctrine is seen in the sorrows and perplexities which millions and millions of helpless widows have for many generations suffered, because they were charged by the families of their husbands, and were often believed by themselves, to have been the cause of the death of their husbands on account of their own sins in a former life.

In contrast with this needless, injurious, unscrupulous theory, there comes into greater relief the Christian doctrine of a holy and living Father, who seeks both by the working of the law of retribution and by the redeeming power of suffering to change the desire and character of the sinning soul, by holding up new ideals and by granting power to overcome the defects of the past. According to the Christian doctrine, "not by being born again into some sinful world, but by being born anew, here and now, through the divine Spirit does the soul rise to a higher and purer life." Not by metaphysical union with an impersonal and supreme It, but by spiritual union with a personal God, and thus by becoming in its measure like God is the full development of the soul to be attained according to Christian teaching.

The Hindu word for union with the Supreme is "Yoga." While meditation and concentration of thought is the highest way to secure Yoga, yet austerities and self-repression are taught to be the principal way by which concentration of thought can be secured. So strange have been the teachings of Hinduism in regard to the method of Yoga that, if thoroughly followed, those efforts result in idiocy. They are thus described by one who has long lived in India. "Yoga is a state of perfect hibernation, in which a Yogi is insensible to heat and cold, to pleasure and pain. . . . It is a total suspension of the function of respiration and circulation." That is, it is finally a state of practical unconsciousness. But such a union with the Supreme is not to develop one's self to the utmost, but to extinguish one's self to the utmost. Moreover, the result to be gained is some assumed benefit to the individual himself. In no wise is it to make the individual helpful to others. So that, as has been said, the Hindu asks, "What shall I do that I may inherit personal extinction of life?" The Christian asks, "What shall I do that I may inherit eternal life?" Christ said, "I am come that men might have life and might have it abundantly."

Comparison between Hinduism and Christianity leads to the final contrast that in Christianity the knowledge of God is for all men by a way which can be understood and followed by all men. All types of popular Hinduism make the way of salvation one of hard works, in which one gains his end by piling up deeds of merit. The Vedantic or higher system lays down the most difficult process which requires a knowledge of metaphysical problems that the unlearned masses can never understand or follow. For the many the way of salvation is a gross, material way. For the favored few the highest way is the way of speculation. And yet the Hindu heart has responded to God's teaching that neither by the way of deeds nor by the way of knowledge does one come into right relations with God, but by the way of grace through humble trust in Him. Only this way of devotion and faith (*bhakti*) is not accompanied by that revelation of God which Jesus Christ has made. As He becomes more and more known to our Hindu brother-men He meets that dim sense of hope which is satisfied by the Christ.

There is but one science for the universe, which we know is and must be true in every land and for every people, whether they understand it or not. There cannot be one astronomy true for India and not for the West: nor one geology, nor one chemistry, nor one psychology true for one part of the world and untrue for another part. Similarly because there is only one God who is evermore the same, all-controlling in every land and in every human heart, there can be but one true moral system. The fatherhood of God and the brotherhood of man make it certain that there is but one moral and spiritual reign, though the embodiment of this reign will vary in form. Religion deals with universal problems relative to God and man, and man's duty to God and other men. So the universal religion will be that which treats all men as the children of one God, who deals with them on the same principle. But the universal religion will be one of universal principles, not one of rules. It will recognize that men must differ and should differ on points of speculation, on ceremonials, and rituals. If, as we believe, Christianity is the fullest interpretation of universal religion which has yet been made, and if it is a growing religion in which there is room for all fuller knowledge that may come to mankind, and is one which adapts itself to various races and individuals according to their individual and varying needs, then Christianity as now developing and to be developed hereafter, will become the religion of India and of the world. Prof. E. W. Hopkins, successor of Prof. W. D. Whitney, of Yale, after visits to India and after exceptional study of the religions of India, thus speaks in his book on "The Religions of India": "In her own religions there is no hope for India, and her best minds have renounced them. The body of Hinduism is corrupt, its soul is evil. As for Brahmanism—the Brahmanism that produced the Upanishads—the spirit is departed and the form that remains is dead." In a spirit of fairness and sympathy, as Christian teachers set forth to the men of India how Jesus Christ best fills out those phases of truth through which they have thought of God in the past, and brings them into helpful and filial relations with Himself, the men of India will come to accept Him more and more as their great Guru. It was the religious men and women of India among others whom our Lord had in mind when He said, "Other sheep I have, which are not of this fold: them also I must bring, and they shall hear my voice; and they shall become one flock, one shepherd."

VI

WHAT CHRISTIANITY HAS TO GAIN FROM CONTACT WITH THE EAST

WHILE the sun draws the earth toward itself, the earth also in the ratio of its bulk draws the sun toward itself. As in physics, so in morals, it is now known that action and reaction are ever at work; that contacts of thought bring modifications in both directions. The larger and weightier thought of course has the greater influence, but the receiver of thought and life also affects the giver. That reaping follows sowing, and giving brings returns, is God's inspiring universal law. And the more unselfishly, and the more without thought or hope of reward that one works for others, the larger and more blessed his reward. "Give and it shall be given unto you; good measure, pressed down, shaken together, running over shall they give into your bosom." The enemy has sometimes sown tares. But as Christianity has been a sower of the good seed of spiritual truth and of loving service to men, so it must in the past have reaped and must hereafter reap bountifully. It has given some of its best men and women from the very first to take to others its own best possession, the truth and love of God as revealed in Jesus Christ. It has spent immense labor in translating the Bible into the manifold tongues of earth. It has cared for the bodies, as well as the spirits, of God's children. It has provided hundreds of thousands of educational opportunities for the minds of non-Christian fellowmen. We can see from the past some of the blessings which have come to Christianity through missionary contact with other faiths. We can forecast some blessings which are still to come. Contact with various peoples through missionary activity has always brought to the church enlargement in thought, in sympathy, and in joy. Enlargement in all directions to the uttermost capacity is necessary for its universality. Because Christianity is a growing religion and thereby has fitness to meet the universal needs of all men it has been, and still is, the principal missionary religion of the world.

Consider how at the very outset the contact of Christianity with non-Christians resulted in an enlargement of vision. While the earliest Christians recognized Jesus Christ as the Messiah, they had the contracted idea of all Jews that salvation is of the Jews and for the Jews. That narrow belief could not have been enlarged in any way save through the logic of missionary activity. Christ had taught His disciples that He was to be the founder of a universal faith and had bidden them carry the Gospel to the uttermost parts of the earth. But none of these teachings had been apprehended by the disciples. On a housetop in Joppa, Peter had seen the vision by which God tried to teach him that He had spiritual children other than Jews, whom He accepted and whom He wished to bless. But Peter did not and could not understand the vision till the exigency of missionary service actually brought him into contact with the devout non-Christian. Then only he received through experience an understanding of the enlarging truth which an intellectual vision had not been able to give. When the apostles and brethren that were in Jerusalem heard this news, instead of praising God they contended with Peter for having lived up to his vision. Though his report of the whole circumstance partly satisfied them, it was not entirely conclusive to the Jerusalem church, for when a Christian movement took place at Antioch there was great opposition to it from the parent church. Again the only evidence that stopped this accusation was the testimony of Peter from his experience as a missionary. Even then how little that Jerusalem church and its leader, James, realized the spirit of the new Christian dispensation is illustrated by the strangely narrow conditions which were enjoined upon the Gentile Christians as essential to their admission to the universal and spiritual religion. Of the four conditions laid down three would not now be thought of in a letter from a missionary society to a community in a foreign land which was wishing to come into Christian fellowship, viz., first, that the new converts must never purchase or use things bought in a market which might previously have been offered to idols; second, must not use blood; and, third, must not eat things strangled. The fourth was the only condition which has a universal ethical character, viz., that the new converts must abstain from fornication. Still again it was the conclusiveness of a visit of Gentiles from Cyprus and Cyrene who had come to accept Jesus as Lord that probably led Barnabas to get an enlarged understanding of the scope of Christianity and led him to become a missionary. Preëminently it was missionary work which helped the conservative Saul to become the interpreter of Christianity as the universal religion. Until he had been induced by Barnabas to leave Tarsus for missionary work at Antioch, there is little to show that Paul had come to understand the universality of the Christian evangel. But when the exigencies of the situation required him to teach and act, then in a masterly way he realized and expounded that in Christ there can be neither Greek nor Jew, circumcision nor uncircumcision, barbarian nor Scythian, bondman nor freedman; for in Christ Jesus those who once were afar off are made nigh, for He is their peace; He made both one, and broke down the middle wall of partition; that through Him all men might have access in one Spirit unto the faith. It was through the implications and requirements of missionary work that Paul was made the first great interpreter of Christ as the reconciler of all men to God, and therefore of Christianity as necessarily the universal religion. And the enlargement which came to him was not only intellectual breadth of vision, but increase of sympathy, of tact, of courage, and of indomitable perseverance in the advocacy and in the spread of Christian truth. It is probable that had some "pent-up Utica" like Tarsus retained him, the history of Christianity would have been far different. The world might have had to wait long for an interpreter of the universality and the liberty that is in Christ Jesus. Through missionary activity the same enlargement of vision and of capacity came to the Antioch church and long made it one of the centers of Christian thought and life, while the mother church soon faded into insignificance because it was not a missionary body and had not a sense of the universality of the Christian religion and of responsibility for making it universal. The same result befell all the non-missionary churches of apostolic times.

It is a commonplace of church history that Christianity has always been greatly influenced by the peoples with whom it has come into contact. The Jewish Christians, like all Jews, were not philosophical. But when Christian principles came into contact with the philosophical Greek world, how many types of Christianity were more or less tinged with or controlled by Greek philosophy. In the New Testament writings the Gospel of St. John is a most striking example. This fourth Gospel is the work of a disciple under the influence of the Alexandrian philosophy, which interpreted the Lord Jesus Christ in the way most effective to commend Him to those who held the eternal *logos* as the principal means of spiritual revelation. The Alexandrian school of Christian theology, which under Clement and Origen was especially influenced by contact with Greek philosophy, was the principal missionary influence in the third century by discerning and proclaiming the points of affinity between the best utterances of non-Christian sages and the teachings of the New Testament. Despite some fanciful allegories and crudities, those early Christian philosophers enlarged the true religion by attempting to place it in an intelligible relation to other religious systems, and to God's purpose in the whole movement of history. When Christianity went into imperial Rome, its type of theology, its mode of worship, and especially its ecclesiastical system and methods were unavoidably and thoroughly Romanized. The Christianity which went into the Greek world had been Jewish. But a Greek environment developed the phases and formative principles of Christ's teachings into that type of Christianity which is called the Greek theology and the Greek church; and on the whole, Christianity gained thereby. The Roman environment brought some gain and some loss to Christianity by creating that type of our religion which is called the Latin theology and the Roman Church.

Modern times furnish illustrations of the same phenomenon. What a contracted outlook was held by the Christians of Great Britain a little over a century ago! What a different man the missionary motive and missionary service made of William Carey, the cobbler! What a quickening came to the churches through his going as a missionary to India! Vision and life came to the man himself, and to the churches which sent him out. How much David Livingstone gained in soul and in influence from his contact with life among the degraded peoples of Africa! What would he have been, and what would the churches of Great Britain have lost, had he stayed in some small sphere in Scotland! In theology, as well as in sympathy, that contact with ethnic principles and faiths which came through the modern missionary movement has immensely helped the churches of Great Britain and America. They once largely held the doctrine of a limited atonement. But as the missionary spirit spread, the logic of the heart made the churches at first secretly, and then more openly, appreciate that there are and that there can be no uncovenanted mercies of God, as had been held. The vision of the countless masses of non-Christian fellowmen going into outer darkness could not continue to be borne or believed. So contact with the people of ethnic faiths has been one prominent influence in leading the advanced churches of Christendom to discard the restriction of

God's saving love to those who intelligently accept Jesus Christ as Saviour and Lord. Probably no one thing now causes more dislike to foreign missions among large numbers of the best Christians in evangelical churches than the supposition that the average missionary believes and teaches to non-Christians that there is no salvation except for those who definitely express their faith in Christ as Saviour. An appeal for support of missions on such a score would doubtless have the opposite effect, and would kill missionary interest in thousands of churches now.

Contact of Christianity with the better sections of the non-Christian world has created even in Christendom a higher and better thought of God. As Peter's first contact with a devout non-Christian made him see and say, "I am finding out that God is greater and better than I had supposed, for I now perceive that God is no respecter of persons; but among every nation he that feareth Him and worketh righteousness is acceptable to Him," so a large body of Christians at heart now believe, whatever the implications of some old standards may be. This larger view of God increases, not lessens, the valuation of Christ as the supreme revelation of God in man, and the importance of making Him known to all men. It increases the appreciation of the spiritual greatness and power of Jesus Christ, because He is now recognized as being the human expression of the larger God. An increased reverence for Christ comes through seeing how the non-Christian world bows in reverence before Him, and by the vision of Him is drawn to *bhakti, i. e.*, reverential love for Him and for the God whom He makes so real and near. Christendom is to get a still greater reverence for the Lord Jesus Christ by seeing how He draws all men to Him, in accordance with His prophetic word, "If I be lifted up, I will draw all men unto me." It would be a revelation to multitudes in the West if they could know how much the words of the Lord Jesus Christ are read and reverenced and meditated on by non-Christians in India; and how He is loved and trusted and followed and even prayed to there. Not a few "Lives of Christ" have been written by Hindus who do not call themselves Christians. "The Oriental Christ," by Pratap Chundar Moozoomdar, is probably the best known of these books. Reverent commentaries on the Gospels of St. Matthew and of St. John have been recently written by a Hindu in Ceylon named Pārananda. The book entitled, "Precepts of Jesus," written so long ago as 1820 by the founder of the Brahma Samāj, Rajah Rammohun Roy, was given to the Hindus by that gifted theistic reformer because he said that the moral code of the New Testament and the teachings of Jesus were the best he knew. He even studied Hebrew and Greek in order that he might satisfy himself that he rightly understood the teachings of the spiritual leader of Christendom. The most gifted and influential Hindu of the immediate past, Justice M. G. Ranade, told me that one principal pursuit of his had been the study of what had made Paul the man he was. Mr. Ranade did not tell me what the conclusion of his study had been, but it seems inevitable that a man of his acumen and judicial habits could not have failed to see that the two things which had made Paul the man whose writings have unquestionably influenced the world more than the writings of any other man, were, first, the vision of Christ, and, second, his own missionary service.

As the West comes more fully to know the history of the ethnic faiths, it will more and more see that those faiths are earlier types from which Christianity has been exempt, or above which it has been gradually raised. Take, for example, the whole theory and practice of sacrifice. Not even in the religion of Israel was there so much required by sacrifice as in the religious development of Hinduism. There was a time when the altars and temples of India ran with blood. Even human sacrifice, as well as the sacrifice of the nobler animals, such as the horse and the cow, were more or less required. But under God's continual teaching of His Indian children, the grosser sacrificial system has largely passed away. There seems to have come, first through Buddhism, a very great restraint to all kinds of animal sacrifice; and at present only in comparatively few places and to a very limited extent are animal sacrifices practiced in India. Does not this plain, historical fact show how God is confirming by new and vivid illustrations the great Christian revelation that God

Himself makes the supreme sacrifice for men? Instead of asking them for a sacrifice to appease Him, the only sacrifice which He desires from His human children is the sacrifice of loving service for brother-men.

I believe that the contact of the East with Christianity will enrich the apprehension of God in the West. In India, when anyone wishes to express affection and trust toward one who is above him, be it man or woman, it is common to say to such, "You are my father and mother." It does not seem enough to say, "You are my father," or "You are my mother." It is felt that full appreciation of love, and tenderness, and power from and toward such a benefactor can only be expressed by calling him or her both father and mother. A similar habit of devout and grateful worship in India is to call God both father and mother. This is frequent in the *abhangs* or lyrics of Tukaram, the popular religious poet of western India. The Roman Catholic practice of reverence for the mother of Jesus, almost like reverence for a divine being, shows a somewhat similar feeling in the human heart of many in the West. It may be that some of the men and women and children of Christendom, too, may find enrichment in their thought and apprehension of God and in communion with Him by thinking and speaking of Him as "Father and Mother."

Contact of Christianity with the peoples of the East is going to enrich Christianity by showing that the evidence of spiritual truth is not so dependent on history as Christians of the West have been inclined to believe. Unquestionably the East is weak in appreciation of the valuation of historical evidence. This characteristic deficiency has over and over again led them into accepting the unreal for the real, and into following moral will-o'-the-wisps. On the other hand, the West is unquestionably weak in over-emphasizing the importance of historicity as almost the only evidence of truth. But the most accurate account of the past can only show us what has been, not what may be or should be. Necessary and valuable as history is, do we go to chroniclers or to poets for the purpose of seeing spiritual laws and the beauties and possibilities of spiritual things? By historical evidence the highest Christianity cannot be verified. Some Christians question the historicity of the virgin birth of Jesus. Suppose that doctrine to be absolutely and unimpeachably accepted as history, how much does that add to the spiritual helpfulness of the Lord Jesus Christ? The Gospels of St. Mark and St. John and the letters of St. Paul make no allusion to it, and therefore do not depend on it. Year by year Christians are finding that scores of points once supposed to be indubitably historical are not such. Yet instead of weakening, this experience has often increased, the spiritual value of Christianity. Will not contact with ethnic faiths in which the ideal is a large part of the evidence on which Orientals rely increase the capacity and readiness of Christians in the West to use the spiritual imagination for the comprehension of spiritual things? The ideal is the best thing in the highest realm. It is the ideal which points the way upward. Faith is seeing the invisible ideal and acting as if it were true. In the parable of Abraham and Lazarus, Jesus Christ said that if men would not believe prophets, *i. e.*, those who announce spiritual things which they have apprehended, then they will not believe even though one rose from the dead. For his time and purpose the apostle Paul rightly emphasized the great importance of the resurrection of Jesus Christ. In 1883, in company with some missionaries in Calcutta I invited the late Keshab Chundar Sen to a conference, in which he frankly spoke to us about his position in regard to some points in the Christian belief. He said that he felt absolutely sure that the spirit of Jesus rose from the dead. He did not know and did not care whether His body also rose or not. And he said that Hindus as a whole would never care. He also implied that he did not know or care whether the Lord Jesus is metaphysically divine or not. He reverenced and loved and followed Him because He was ethically and spiritually divine. On these grounds Keshab said that the object of his life was to lead his countrymen to Christ. It is the character of Christ, and the ideal quality of His teachings, not His resurrection from the dead, which draws the East toward Him. When the East says that it is satisfied that the spirit of Jesus rose and does not care whether

His body rose or not, and that through such confidence it accepts Him as its spiritual Guide, the one who has brought light and immortality to life through the Gospels, men in the West may come to see that the historicity of the physical resurrection of Jesus is not as essential to Christianity as has sometimes been supposed.

Even in the hard-headed West, metaphysics in the long run is greater than physics. Though blunter and more material methods of demonstration sometimes seem to have put metaphysics aside, the latter has a way of luring men to depend on it. Just now in the realm of thought metaphysics is receiving much more attention and valuation than half a generation ago. So when the East, with its gift for metaphysics, joins the West, with its gift for history, we may expect in the Church become universal among all races that balanced judgment which will give an estimate and interpretation of spiritual things to which the Occidental Church has not yet attained. How strange to the Eastern mind, even before it wholly bows before the Lord Jesus Christ as its spiritual Master, is the marked tendency in some quarters by the most exact, critical, and historical study, to limit to that which is indubitably shown by documents to have been spoken by Jesus the acceptance of anything as truly from Him and as legitimately expressing Him and His teaching! The "historical Christ" has become a phrase of considerable usage. It is assumed that only from those words which the historical Christ certainly spoke can we ascertain what is Christian. The spiritual interpretations of their Master by His greatest disciples, such as St. Paul and the writer of the fourth Gospel, are discounted by a class of thinkers. But Christianity will never become a universal religion on such a basis as that. If Greek philosophy and metaphysics molded that type of Christianity which has always controlled the Greek section of the church, and if Greek theology is now helping the Western Church to modify the Latin theology which was so long dominant, then Oriental ways of thinking are going still more to influence and to fertilize the thinking and the life of Christendom in the West.

One of the glaring weaknesses of Christendom has been the tendency to reserve certain spheres of life for religion and to term the rest secular. In some ethnic faiths, certainly in Hinduism, there has been no such weakness. Every least detail of thought and life from before the birth till after the death of the individual has been rightly deemed as something religious. Also religion is there considered not mainly a matter of individual concern: it is preëminently a social consideration. Herein is one chief power of caste. Caste is practically the living religion of India. And it exercises power because as religion it expresses the right relation between man and the Supreme, and between man and man. So it masterfully controls the everyday life of Hindus. Contact with such ethnic faiths is going to strengthen the tendency among Western Christians to make religion here include every department of life and every feature of every department. It will be a sound element of the "Back-to-Christ" movement when we believe as well as say, "Whether ye eat or drink, or whatsoever ye do, do all to the glory of God." Such a belief and practice is essential for making Christianity universal: universal in its application to every single detail of the life of every man as well as of all men everywhere.

Again, in the West there is a tendency to esteem the substance of any matter, entirely apart from its form, as the only important consideration. In the East, form is deemed an essential part of every matter. It is not enough to have a good thing. Its goodness depends considerably on the way in which it is administered and is received. An Oriental monarch once had a dream and asked one of his wise men to interpret the dream. The man said, "The meaning of your dream is this: Your children will die, and then you will die." This blunt and untactful reference to the possibility of death caused the monarch to order the immediate beheading of that interpreter. He then asked another courtier for the interpretation of the dream, who said, "The meaning of your Majesty's dream is this: Your Majesty will survive his children." This interpreter received reward and honor. The story is not without significance for men in the West. Will not contact with peoples and faiths of the East strengthen a conviction in Christendom that refinement and appreciation of the best way of doing things is a necessary part of true religion. What is culture which people in the West are coming more and more to value, except a higher and higher valuation of the importance of doing everything in the best way? The principal thing which Orientals dislike in Occidentals is their bluntness in the relations of life; their occasional rudeness through disregard of those civilities and courtesies which constitute one chief charm of life. Even in America the word Christian is by no means a synonym for gentleman. This weakness makes some people in some cultured but not deeply religious circles seek more to be gentlemen than Christians and thereby to plume themselves on being all that they ought to be. Contact of Christianity with the ethnic peoples and faiths will bring to Western Christianity an added conviction that the most courteous way of doing things is an important virtue, pleasing to God, and is the truly Christian way of manifesting those relations to brother-men which are according to the spirit of Christ.

Allied to this point is the difference of estimate and of development of the virtue of reverence in Christendom and among Eastern peoples. Who does not know that the civilization of the West is weak in regard to appreciating and developing this high quality on which so much depends in the relations of the family, of the school, and of the whole framework of society, as well as of religion? Here the imagination has not been properly cultivated. There is no adequate veneration for the old and for the past. Our places of worship can be entered with hats on the head. Everyone feels authorized and able to criticise every opinion which he hears, and to criticise every person whom he meets or knows about. Perhaps among the Chinese the feeling of veneration for the past, for ancestors and elders, has the highest development. But it is a sterling virtue also in Japan and in India. The Christian religion is not the cause of this deficiency in the West. We are weak because we are not as Christian as we ought to be. Yet probably even in the New Testament reverence is not so much dwelt on as in some non-Christian sacred books. "A

Hindu philosopher, casting a glance at a beautiful flower, with which he might worship his deity, asks, 'How can I bring myself to pluck it, seeing that it is Thyself that is there?'" He connects the flower with his god.

The Hindu type of religion is meditative and reflective. The Western type is active and seeks to serve God by serving one's fellowmen. It is a splendid type, which makes the wilderness to bud and blossom as the rose. The Orient greatly needs to copy and assimilate the Occidental type of true piety. But equally does the West need to copy the quiet, thoughtful, meditative type of the East. It can best be accomplished through contact with the East. In theory the Christian Church places the character of Mary before that of Martha: in practice it lives as if Martha, not Mary, had chosen the better part.

As Christianity has developed in the West, it has been a mixture of Christian practices with some non-Christian ideas of the peoples who accepted it. Its leaders are more and more seeking to know its essentials; to recognize at their true worth things that are not fundamental, and to cast out those elements which are inconsistent with the simplicity that is in Christ Jesus. Dogmatism about denominational peculiarities and ecclesiastical arrangements and non-essentials is being counted as at variance with the Christian spirit. Contact with ethnic faiths will, through comparison and differentiation, help in securing an analysis of the very essence of Christianity, and in understanding that the essentials of the Christian religion are certain spiritual and ethical conceptions of God and of man, especially as revealed by Jesus, and certain principles and motives of action which enable men to attain to that character which the character of God calls for. Under past historical conditions, with certain philosophical pre-suppositions there have been produced certain institutions and theologies which have borne the Christian name. Growing knowledge of non-Christian religions is showing that, as under different sociological conditions and on different philosophical assumptions, certain non-Christian institutions and theologies have been produced, so, even after contact with Christianity under the sociological conditions and the philosophical assumptions of the Orient, somewhat different types of Christianity will be developed there. A combination of all types can alone give complete universality to Christianity. Christianity is a growing religion, which is now the religion of the more advanced peoples and which has for its inspiring base the belief in the fatherhood of God and the brotherhood of man. Therefore it has the inspiring missionary motive of brotherliness and of responsibility, both of imparting to all men that which it has received from God, and of receiving from all men that which God has taught them. Therefore it must be and will be universalized. As it will impart to men of other faiths the things of supremest value which it has received, it will receive from them whatever they may have to give.

The life has gone out of other religions. Hear the words of a Hindu leader looking at the condition of his own religion: "There is no more tragic event under the sun than the death of a nation, and this consists in the destruction of peoples and institutions and national peculiarities that give it an individual character.

This awful tragedy is now going on in India. The old religion is dying, the old morality is dying; the bonds of custom and tradition, which are the bones and sinews of the social organism, are dissolving; there is death and decomposition all around." When the old Greek and Roman religions were similarly dying, the first great Christian missionary made their best elements live again in higher Christian forms, and thus enabled them to do even more for the world than they had done before. The Greek thinkers had sought for truth, for beauty, for freedom, and for the highest ideals of life. As these nations and philosophies were passing away, Paul, by his interpretation of Christ as their highest fulfillment, made their spirit live forever by passing them into those Christian institutions and theologies which had the dynamic of Christ in them. Without Christ, those ideals would not have been fulfilled. Without those ideals, the Christianity of Paul and of the whole church would not have been as rich as it became. In his letter to the Romans, Paul rightly taught that even the Old Testament shows that national blessings had been bestowed on the Jews that through them all men might be blessed; and that every good element in individual and national life attains perfection only when it is caught up in, and developed into, a larger whole. God has made of one every nation of men to dwell on all the face of the earth.* This does not mean to dwell in uniformity of rite and dogma: but it does mean in unity of the spirit in relation to God. The history of modern thought and life under the continuous tutelage of God is a record of the good and of the permanent, mixed with the evil and the transient. St. Paul's explanation of the mystery by which the good is being separated from the bad is by God's revelation of that mystery as a dispensation of the fullness of the times by summing up of all things in Christ. All things are to be summed up in Him. No good thing is to be lost. In Him all things hold together. In Him all fullness becomes permanent. Bishop Westcott has put this inspiring assurance in the following words: "Vast peoples, richly endowed with manifold gifts, still remain without the pale of the faith. These may even now be being disciplined for some future work. The races of the Far East,

* Rev. A. Crosthwaite, in *Harvest Field.*

we can hardly doubt, will in their season lay open fresh depths of the Gospel which we are unfitted to discover. Already there are symptoms of such a consummation: and when once we trust the simple apostolic message, we shall be allowed to learn as we have never yet done how it can take up and transfigure the most different forms of conduct and thought and become more glorious as it does so." The author of the Epistle to the Hebrews expresses this hope by saying that God had foreseen some better things for Christians of later times, that without the saints whom Christ is later enlightening, even the leaders of the faith in the past should not be made perfect. And St. Paul says that Christ's work of perfecting the saints will go on till we all—not only all individuals, but all races—attain unto the unity of the faith and the knowledge of the only God, unto full grown men, unto the measure of the fullness of Christ. Bishop Gore expresses the same hope thus: "Each new race which is introduced into the Church not only itself receives the blessing of our religion, but reacts upon it to bring out new and unsuspected aspects and beauties in its truth and influence. It has been so when Greeks, and Latins, and Teutons, and Kelts, and Slavs have each in turn been brought into the growing circle of believers. How impoverished was the exhibition of Christianity which the Jews were capable of giving by themselves! How much the treasures of wisdom and power which lie hid in Christ awaited the Greek intellect, and the Roman spirit, and the Teutonic individuality, and the temper and character of the Kelt and Slav, before they could leap into light! Can we doubt that now again not only would Indians, and Japanese, and Africans, and Chinamen be the better for Christianity, but that Christianity would be unspeakably also richer for their adhesion—for the gifts which the subtlety of India, and the grace of Japan, and the silent patience of China are capable of bringing into the city of God?"

The true Christian position is not that that apprehension of Christ which has already been attained by any one church, or any one race, is the full apprehension of all that the Lord Jesus Christ truly is. It is the faith that as in the past God has through His Son progressively revealed more and more of Himself, so He will continue to do through the bringing of all humanity into union with that Son, and through Him into union with Himself. Just as in the past the various races have in their own way added something to the revelation of the unsearchable riches of Christ, so in the future every race will, by its thought and life, apprehend and reveal riches in Christ which the Western nations need also to apprehend. I suppose that the Japanese recognize and admit that the unexpected capacity and power which they are manifesting in their present contest with Russia are in some measure due to their contact with even the partial Christianity of the West. And what shall the unsearchable riches of Christ prove to be when

"Every creature, every tribe
On this terrestrial ball,
To Christ all majesty ascribe,
And crown Him Lord of all."

VII

THE SIMPLICITY OF CHRISTIANITY

THERE is a large number of men in India who have a fair knowledge of the English language and who have come somewhat into contact with the current literature and thought of the West. The major part of such persons have lost faith in the indigenous religions of their country without acquiring in their stead any intelligent and vital religious thought and life for themselves. Some of them have read and heard some of the objections in the West to a part of traditional Christian theology. They easily imagine that there is little certitude about any Christian positions. In conversation with missionaries they would prefer to follow the critical spirit which they have acquired and through which they have lost confidence in their former faiths. They would like to discuss those Western objections to traditional theology about which they have some hazy conception. But the wise missionary knows that thought and talk in this direction are not for the spiritual good of such unsettled men. By race these men are still religious. He would like to lead them into personal communion with the Lord Jesus Christ and through Him to help them to gain true spiritual life. In order to do this he should avoid reference to those matters which are the staple of current objections in the West. Otherwise he would himself immediately lead the conversation on to topics which his visitors would greedily follow. He should confine himself, so far as possible, to the most simple and vital matters. If he can speak largely in the way in which he thinks that Christ Himself would direct the conversation, he would be following his Master. The following statement is an example of the way in which I often give to such men the good news of life in God through the Lord Jesus Christ.

There are many thoughtful people in India like you who are greatly drawn to Jesus Christ, who recognize the beauty and power of His life and teaching, who are thereby being helped in their own lives, who are not following any Indian religion, who do not consider themselves Christians, who are perplexed by the varieties among Christians, and who would like to know what is the simple, essential thing in Christianity. From my own experience and from the testimony of the best Christian literature and of the best Christians I will tell you frankly and simply what the essence of Christianity is and what good it is to be a real Christian.

The first point is that even in Christian countries in all branches of the Christian Church there is search for agreement as to what is the essential thing in Christianity. Both in Europe and America conferences are constantly taking place among members of different denominations, articles are constantly appearing in the religious press, asking what is the characteristic, indispensable truth which every Christian holds and must hold. The best minds everywhere candidly say that the essential thing in Christianity is much less than all the creed and practice of any branch of the church.

This tendency is largely due to God's providence in teaching His children in many things outside of religion. In all science, in all practical life men are seeking first to know what the facts are, what the primal elements and principles are. Similarly under God's guidance His Christian children are seeking to understand clearly what the primal elements and principles of Christianity are. Theology is an explanation or philosophical statement of the facts which Christianity presents. Just as the science of astronomy is changing, not because the facts of astronomy have changed, but because new facts are constantly becoming known, so the science of Christian theology must be modified, when new religious facts become known, and their relation to old facts become better understood. Moreover, just as in all science an important distinction is carefully made between facts on the one hand, and laws, doctrines, hypotheses and so on on the other hand, so in theology an important distinction is now made between the essential facts of Christianity and the inferences from those facts, some of which are very generally acknowledged as Christian doctrines, and others of which inferences are more or less controverted.

This scientific, careful, truth-seeking tendency

is helping men to recognize what is the characteristic essential thing in Christianity. For example, everyone, non-Christian as well as Christian, knows that there is a book called the Bible. That is a fact. There have been innumerable discussions over *how* the Bible came to be, and with what kind and degree of divine assistance it was written. That inquiry is right. Thinking men must have some theory about all important matters. But that inquiry is not the essential thing about the Bible. The essential thing is what does the Bible say? what facts of religious significance does it disclose? Since it tells many wonderful, helpful things about God, all Christians believe that God in some way helped the writers of the Bible in their work. This is the simplest position of Christianity about the Bible.

However, though all Christians thus recognize the Bible as at least the principal *record* of many most important facts in the religious history of mankind and as written by God's help, yet it is not the Bible which is the characteristic, essential thing in Christianity. The characteristic thing in Christianity is that which gives it its name, viz., Christ. Christ is Christianity, and the supreme simplicity of this religion is that it can truly be so summed up. Hence, loyalty to Christ is the one peculiar requisite of the Christian. Therefore, following Him, in some way or other taking His help all the time in our lives, is being a Christian.

Now what does loyalty to Christ mean and imply, and how is it to be carried out? Let us ask Him. On one occasion some women brought their children to Jesus Christ, hoping that in some way He would help them. Christ's disciples, who up to that time understood Him very imperfectly, imagined that such a religious teacher would not have much for children, and therefore began to drive away the women. But when Jesus saw this He was much displeased and said, "Let the children come to me, because of such is the kingdom of God. Whoever does not come to God like a little child cannot know God or be in His kingdom." This was a characteristic teaching of Christ, and it shows how He expects men now to get acquainted with Him, and then to become loyal to Him. The childlike way of knowing anyone is not to read a book about him or read arguments about him, but to see him, hear him, go about with him, and by such personal intercourse to get acquainted, and then to trust and love such a person. In other words the childlike way is the vital way, the way of life, in fact, the way in which we all truly come to know anything. How can one learn carpentry and get help from some skillful carpenter? It is essential to find out from the testimony of some person or book or paper that there is such a carpenter, where he lives, and how others have received help from him. But this is only preliminary. This alone would not enable a young man to learn carpentry from that carpenter. The one simple, essential thing is to go to that carpenter and stay with him and follow his directions. That is the simple, vital way which Christ always points out as the one by which men can get His help. As before, so now He always says, " Come and see," " Learn of me," " Follow me," " Take my help." That was the one way in which His first disciples came to know Him and grew to be loyal to Him. The ordinary name which they used in speaking to Him and of Him was "Master," *i. e.*, Teacher. The *only* name given to His followers in the four gospels is "disciples," *i. e.*, scholars. They learned from Him about Himself and many other things by associating with Him, seeing more and more who He was, and gradually they grew more and more loyal to Him. Before His death and resurrection and spiritual presence they could not adequately understand Him. But after those experiences they grew more and more loyal to Him and had higher and higher appreciation of Him.

We, too, in India can get properly acquainted with Him and become truly loyal to Him only in this same simple, vital way. At first sight this might seem impossible because He is not physically visible to men. But this is not at all so. In fact there are some special advantages which we now have over those first disciples.

In the first place, we must remember that the resurrection of Jesus Christ assures us not simply that He *once* rose from the dead—that alone would be a matter of small moment. The great, the important assurance is that He is *now alive* and ever will be alive, and, since He is now in a more spiritual, glorified sphere, it is easier for every man everywhere to associate with Him and get His help. In the second place, we now have a much completer view of Christ than those who had seen His physical form. We now make small account, as they could not, of His physical limitations. This absence of physical appearance *aids* us in emphasizing His spiritual teachings and life. Moreover, we have those interpretations of Him which have come from His most spiritual followers, such as Paul and John and others. We have the revelation and interpretation of Him which have come from the best experiences of His church and from history. All this is a very great help. Finally, we know that the best part of any man is his spirit, *i. e.*, his thoughts, his aspirations, his loves. Physical intercourse, even with a great man, is often a hindrance to one's getting the most help from his spirit. The biographies of great men furnish many illustrations of this. Now the New Testament contains very few references to the body of Jesus Christ. It is full of His spirit. That is what we want. And if He is now seeking for spiritual intercourse with us, then with the help of those spiritual revelations which are in the New Testament we can now have spiritual fellowship with Him, we can learn who He is for us, how He helps, whether to be loyal to Him or not, and how.

It is feasible now for you or for any man to learn of Him in the simple, vital way of personal intercourse. You can yourself see how this can be done. The intercourse of the vast majority of officials and employees in India to-day is through writing. Living men who work every day under the same roof impart and receive directions mainly through writing. Though they may see one another with physical sight, their personal intercourse is mainly spiritual, not physical. Now this kind of spiritual intercourse with Jesus Christ is just as feasible for every man as with his superintendent or employer. When a subordinate gets written directions from his superior, at first sight he may not wholly understand them. Then what does he do? He might go directly and ask for explanations. If he did, probably his superior would say: "If you do not understand it all, never mind now. Begin and follow the directions carefully step by step, and it will all come out straight and plain. Those are the very same directions which have been given in this office for years, and have been found to be sufficient. However, if you get into difficulty, why come to me and I will then explain whatever is necessary." For essence, Jesus Christ says not only that, but something more helpful. He says: "I have given you some written directions; but knowing how easy it is for men who are weak and not spiritual to misunderstand spiritual principles, to go astray, and to get discouraged, confused, and more weak, I am not leaving you alone to work out your own salvation. The Holy Spirit of God, whose special work it is to explain spiritual things and to help men to attain them, will stay with you night and day and will enable you both to know and to do what you need. What you have to do is to speak with Him and with Me, to expect and to follow our guidance."

Now let me say to you what I would say to a man in America who wished for personal intercourse with Jesus in a simple, intelligible way so as actually to find out by his own experience what Christ can do for him. I would say to such a man that he can begin almost anywhere. The natural place would be at some point where the man feels some need, especially some spiritual need. And beginning anywhere, the first thing to do is not to ask Christ to show us what to do, but to watch Him and see how He lived, how He did the thing in which we are weak. Just as the first thing to do for one who wishes to learn carpentry from a carpenter is not to ask questions, but to watch the carpenter. Suppose a man wants to find out what Christ can do to help him to become truthful.* Absolute truthfulness is a fundamental, but a very rare virtue.

A man who wants to become a better man knows he is very weak here and needs help. He first reads Christ's life, and notices how absolutely true He was. There was no make-believe, no policy, no shiftiness in Him. So the man would naturally say: "I wish to be like Him. I will at least think of Him, and I will accept whatever help He gives me." Then, thinking of

* Suggestions have been taken from Dr. Newman Smyth's "Personal Creeds."

Christ, constantly reading His life, and looking to Him, he follows truth in everything. He sees that he must begin by being true at heart. He must not deceive himself, or pretend to be what he is not. When he speaks, he seeks to say just what is true. He looks at facts and means to understand them just as they are, not to twist them to mean what he would like them to mean. He finds this kind of being, thinking, speaking, acting, beset with all manner of difficulty. He is all the time falling below the standard of Christ and his own ideal, too. He is making enemies. He is made more and more humble. He finds that some of his bitterest critics are men prominent in religious circles. This surprises him. But it all makes him marvel more and more at the absolute, transparent sincerity of Christ, and more and more to find a satisfaction in humble sincerity and a gradual willingness to suffer the criticisms and persecution which the longing for truthfulness brings. He understands the glory of Christ who was "full of truth," and he finds himself having more and more intercourse with Christ and getting more and more help from Him. And his experience is not that his trying and trying is what enables him to grow in truth, but that his admiration for the spotless truthfulness of Christ and association with Him are making a change in himself.

Longing to be true and following the truth bring so many trials that a man might soon begin to ask how he should treat his enemies; and then in Christ's simple vital way he might go to Christ to find out and to get help. First, he would notice how Christ treated His enemies. He would see that the feeling of revenge seemed absolutely wanting in Christ's conduct toward those who willfully and persistently opposed Him. His feeling was one of mingled indignation and pity: indignation because of their rancor, their hypocrisy, their not simply staying away from Him, but their hindering simple folk from coming to Him: and deep pity because they were spiritually so lean and poor. He would see this spirit manifested all through Christ's life, and finally hear Him pray, as His executioners were nailing Him to the cross, "Father, forgive them, for they know not what they do." And he would find that this thinking of Jesus, associating with Jesus, was gradually making him feel somewhat the same toward his own enemies. He would see that it was not trying to be like Christ, but associating with Christ, which was helping him and really developing Christlikeness in him. It is varied and repeated experiences of this kind which are the practical, convincing proof of Christ and His helpfulness, and which awaken that loyalty to Him which is the essence of Christianity. Personal intercourse with Christ and humbly taking His help, *i. e.*, trusting Him, having faith in Him, have always had two results: first, a higher and higher view of Him; and, second, a vital understanding of how He helps men.

Eighteen centuries ago many men talked about Him, considered His wonderful works, compared them with the works of others, admitted that He was a very extraordinary being, but that was all. They got little or no help from Him. His disciples *lived* with Him, saw much of His personal life, admired Him, followed His teachings, unconsciously were molded by His person, and they got unspeakable help from Him. Toward the end of His public ministry one day Christ asked His disciples, "Who do men say that I am?" They answered, "Some people say that you are one prophet or great religious teacher; others say you are still another prophet; still others say you are a third prophet." Then Jesus asked, "But what do you say?" To this Peter promptly replied with the first distinctively Christian confession, "Thou art the Christ, the Son of the Living God," *i. e.*, "You are the One who makes us know in our very lives and hearts God as living and helpful to men." That is what Christ wants to do, to make men know God as He really is, a living, helpful Father. Therefore instantly He replied to Peter, "Blessed art thou, Peter. You have got what I have to give. It is first on you, and hereafter on men like you, men of like understanding of me, of like faith on me that I found my church." That is the essence of Christianity according to its founder; to use Him as the revelation of a living God, who therefore is like Him, and thus by His help to come into humble filial relations with God our Heavenly Father.

Now let me tell you what the spiritual blessing

is which comes to men through trustful personal intercourse with Christ, and what is the characteristic way by which Christ imparts it to men. Thoughtful men admit that the highest blessing possible to a man is his becoming acceptable to God. But to the question, how man may become acceptable to God, the religions of the world have given different answers. Some say, "Repeat over and over the name of God." Some say, "Practice austerities." Some say, "Perform such and such rites." Others say, "Perform other rites." But, apart from the characteristic way which Christ points out, every other religion practically says that the way for man to become acceptable to God is to work hard, to make sacrifices, and by such efforts to win or earn God's favor. Now, without going into details, it is sufficient to show that all of these other ways are mistaken and inadequate for two reasons: first, because they do not rightly understand what it is that God desires in men, what it is that makes men acceptable to Him; and, second, because they are not able to accomplish in man what is necessary to make him acceptable to God.

In the first place, do you believe that what God really desires in you and in others is to believe something—it matters not what—*about* Him; or desires that you should constantly repeat His name; or that you should practice austerities on your body; or that you should perform a large number of rites and ceremonies; or that you should try, and try very hard, to please Him, and repent when you have failed, and try again, and so on? Certainly it is none of these things that you desire in your wife or child or friend. Then how much less does God desire any of these things from any of His human children. What any wise and good man wants from his children and associates is purity of heart and true love. And that is what God desires in men. According to Jesus only harmony with God, love for Him, makes one acceptable to Him. Some of Jesus' sayings are these: "God is spirit, and they that worship Him must worship Him in spirit and in truth." "Thou shalt love the Lord thy God with all thy heart and with all thy soul and with all thy mind. This is the first and great commandment." Therefore it is a mistake to imagine that what

God desires in us is efforts to make ourselves good. What He wants is our trustful, obedient love.

The second inherent weakness in all proposals to make men acceptable to God by trying and trying, *i. e.*, by works which are supposed to secure more or less of merit, is that these efforts have not power to secure their end. The desired end is purity of heart and humble love for God. But when a man sets out to make himself acceptable to God by works of various kinds, he sooner or later considers that what God really desires is works, works, works; not love and purity of heart. Then, if the man trying to make himself acceptable by works comes even approximately up to his standard, what is the inevitable result? He is satisfied, probably puffed up and proud. And when a man is satisfied with himself or is proud, where is his humility or repentance or purity of heart? Where is his humble love for God? It is himself that he is satisfied with and loves. No other result is possible in a man who thinks to make himself acceptable to God by works and who comes approximately up to his own standard.

But there are some tender souls who set out to make themselves acceptable to God by works, and whose ideal is high, who find themselves constantly falling below their ideal and who find unworthy motives constantly coming in to mar the sincerity and value of their deeds, and who for this reason get discouraged, and who know that they are not acceptable in their own sight, much less in God's sight. So that both in the case of those who think they are succeeding, and in the case of those who know they are not succeeding, the way of trying to become acceptable to God by one's own efforts is not the true, vital way. It is mistaken in aim and inadequate in power. That great spiritual hero, Paul, has given us his testimony on this point. If there ever was a man who tried to make himself acceptable to God by great efforts and good deeds, it was he. But the result of all his efforts was the deepest dissatisfaction with himself and consciousness of failure before God. Describing his experience before he took Christ's help, he said, " I knew what I ought to do and tried and tried to do it; but I always failed. O wretched man! Who could deliver me out of this death!"

But then, going on to tell what a different experience he had after his relation of personal trust in Christ, he said, "I thank God. Jesus Christ does save from such death."

This leads me to explain how a trustful personal relation with Jesus Christ secures the highest spiritual blessing to man, viz., harmony with God. I will not try to explain the whole of the process. I only state in a simple, vital way which you or any man can test, the characteristic essential thing in Christianity. If a boy is a very timorous person living among friends and associates of like character, how can he be made a courageous lad? Will it be by people telling him not to fear, and by his trying not to be afraid? Not at all. The way by which he can become a brave man is by associating with a good and brave man who is willing to help him, and for whom he cannot help feeling respect and love. Living with such a man, seeing how his truthfulness and trust in God and man keep him from fear and make him brave, helps that timorous boy. He finds that in time of trouble his brave friend is always near and always helps, and so he becomes himself a brave man. Or, if a boy is lazy and his mates are lazy, how can he become industrious? Not by people telling him to be industrious, nor simply by his trying to become such. The true way is for him to *live* with some noble, industrious man whose example is always inspiring, and who will take great pains for and with him, who will suffer for him, who will make him sorry for his faults, and who will thus enable him to become a different boy.

In the same way it is *living with Christ* which is the one true way of enabling a sinful man to become acceptable to God. When one does this, the first thing which he notices is the difference between himself and Christ. He sees Christ having an absolute and wholly unselfish love for God his Father, and having spotless purity of character. He sees Christ suffering for the sins of men. He feels Christ longing to free him from his weakness and sins. Love for Christ springs up in his heart. He finds Christ helping him to live better. And by Christ's help he becomes like Christ, and so a different man. By Christ's help he comes into harmony with God. This is an intelligible process which you can understand and can try for yourself. It is the essential thing in Christianity.

For two reasons I will not try to explain to you one central element in the process by which Christ helps men, viz., the part which His sufferings and death have in making sinful men into new creatures. His apostles and followers all make His sufferings and death the center of His influence. The first reason why I do not attempt this is that Christians differ in their explanation, *i. e.*, in their philosophy, of this wonderful truth. Now the philosophy of anything is not a part of the essence of Christianity. The second reason is that, as the first disciples had true vital relations with Christ without any explanation and sometimes with divergent explanations of this great truth, so now men may have and do have helpful relations with Him, while in a similar position in regard to any explanation of the exact force of His sufferings and death. The supreme fact is that Christ reveals God's indignation and sorrow for man's sin, His long-suffering love for man under the chains of sin, and His power to free them from it. No religion gives to repentance the importance and reality which Christ gives it. But undoubtedly repentance must be the beginning of growth in spiritual life, for repentance means dissatisfaction with one's imperfect past, and a humble, earnest desire to do better. But even repentance is not hopeful nor fruitful unless accompanied and strengthened by what we call faith, *i. e.*, confidence in one who is able and glad to help us in our needs, resulting in loving gratitude to the one who renders such help. It is a simple, historical fact and a daily experience of many men that the sufferings and death of Christ make men dissatisfied with their sinful past and anxious to become better, that they quicken faith in Him as able and willing to help, and that they create ardent and grateful devotion to Him. Thus they bring men into helpful relations to Christ. This is the essential thing in Christianity. And those who come into these helpful relations to Christ and live with Him gradually become like Him by the certain laws of the mind.

I will now take a step further and show how such trustful association with Christ enables men to understand and to realize the highest relation to God. In a word, it enables them to live in truly filial relations with Him. Multitudes of people use high religious language which does not express any distinct, conscious experience. It is merely vague phraseology. Many men constantly call God their Father. But no one living with them would have the remotest idea that in their souls those men feel like sons of God, or in their lives live like sons of God. But without a doubt Jesus Christ did do just this. His entire consciousness was that of a son. All His conception of God was the conception of a Father. All His feelings were those of a loving son. So far as we can judge from the gospels, He never spoke to God without addressing Him as Father. Not only so, but He also thought of all men as, according to God's own plan and wish, children of God. Only He knew that they did not so think of themselves, nor live as God's sons, and could not thus live so long as they had low thoughts and ideals and habits—though in their own estimation some of them were very religious people because they did a great many religious acts. But, though men fall below their essential sonship to God, yet because Christ thinks of them as such, His one great work is to enable men to live as sons of God. Among the first words of the account of Christ, which is called the Gospel of John, we find it said, "As many as received Him, to them He gave the right [*i. e.*, the privilege] to become sons of God."

To enable men really to live as sons of God is Christ's supreme work. At first even His disciples could not adequately grasp this conception. So He had to use terms which they could better understand. We can believe that a daughter of our late good Queen Victoria, who was in perfect sympathy with her, might perhaps think of her as Queen-mother without great distinction in the two terms. At any rate to Jesus Christ it must have been that the expression "Kingdom of God," which He so often used, was nearly synonymous with the Fatherhood of God, which expression we do not find in the gospels, very likely because at the time that He was teaching in Palestine it would not have been well understood. Certainly the greater includes the less. Christ's supreme conception of God was that of Father, and so must include the conception of God as King. God's Kingdom is a paternal rule where paternal and filial love are the controlling principles.

Now the blessed thing is that trustful association with Christ enables men to live in such filial relations with their heavenly Father. Christ does this first by being such Himself. He was the Son of God in a peculiarly high sense. Nevertheless, it is true that He is our elder brother, and we are younger sons of the same Father. And He helps His younger brethren to realize what sonship to God is by His own filial relation to that Father. The deepest reverence for that Father, the most absolute conformity to His will, the utmost delight in His service, the most sensitive desire that He should be known and appreciated, in short, spiritual oneness with that Father characterized Him so that He could truly say, "The Father and I are one." This shows His perfectly filial relation to God. Thus seeing Him men can in some measure understand how He was the Son of God. Thereby He gives us a conception of what, in some measure, we may become, and awakens in our hearts a sense of privilege and duty and love. The inherent possibility in man begins to develop into reality.

In the second place, He helps men to become sons of God by telling them that that is God's plan and wish for them. He tells them always to address God as Father. He said, "Whenever you pray, begin thus, 'Our Father'; and while you may freely tell Him every slightest need, remember especially that He knows what is best and will do what is best. Therefore always say, and always mean it, too, 'Thy will be done,' for, after all, what you most need is to know and do and love our Father's will." His teaching might almost be typically condensed in a few other quotations about men's bearing themselves like sons of their Heavenly Father. Here are a few of those teachings: "Be not anxious, saying, What shall we eat? or What shall we drink? or, Wherewithal shall we be clothed? for your heavenly Father knoweth that ye have need of all these things." "If ye then, being evil, know how to give good gifts unto your children, how much more shall your Father which is in heaven give good things to them that ask Him?" "Love your enemies, and pray for them that persecute you, that ye may be sons of your Father who is in heaven." "Ye therefore shall be perfect, as your heavenly Father is perfect."

In the third place, Christ helps men to become sons of God by identifying Himself with them, by being, as He Himself says, *with* them and *in* them, and having them *in* Himself. In mystic language, which is yet intelligible, He tells how He personally associates with and helps those who trustfully associate with Him. For example, He says that such a person is to Him in such a relation as a branch is to a vine. When a branch is in vital union with a vine just such sap as is in the vine comes into the branch and by that living relation that branch has just such leaves and just such fruit as the vine. "In a similar way," He says, "if you will live in me, I will put my sap into you; that is, my thoughts, my beliefs, my aims, my loves, my life will come into you and you will become like me." Now what I am trying to do is to put these truths in a simple, intelligible way which you can test for yourself. Wordsworth has well said, "We *live* by admiration, hope and love." So if any man lives with Christ, he cannot help admiring Him, looking up to Him, gradually living as He does, hoping for higher things, and more and more loving Him. In Wordsworth's language, he lives by admiration, hope, and love for Christ, and so becomes like Christ, and therefore like Him realizes filial relations with his Heavenly Father. This is the essence and the simplicity of Christianity.

It may help you if I specify one or two particulars where the supreme excellence of this simple Christian way manifests itself. The crucial point where every system except the Christian system glaringly shows its weakness is in its inability to secure thorough humility together with other great spiritual attainments. If a man is unusually gifted and hard-working and self-denying and otherwise preëminent, how can he also be kept thoroughly humble? The Christian way secures it by making the comparison—if any comparison is made at all—not between that man and other men, but between that man and Christ, and every such comparison is always and only humbling to the Christian. It is not only that we are following and emulating our Father and elder brother, but that whatever good we may do we do for love to them and by their help. What place then is left for pride? Through such influence the truest Christian is the humblest man.

A second crucial point in ethics is the elevation and soundness of motive in our relations with our fellowmen. Trustful association with Jesus Christ awakens in man motives like His own. His motives were true respect for men—even the most sinful men—because essentially they are sons of God, and the most unselfish love for them as lost sons needing to be saved. The simplicity of Christianity is that trustful association with Christ secures such high relations also with men. I urge you to try this simple, vital way for yourself.

Ever since the few short years of Christ's earthly life in Palestine, nearly nineteen hundred years ago, He has been an invisible person. From the first He Himself recognized that His work of revealing God to men and enabling them to become sons of God was circumscribed by His human, visible condition. So long as He could be seen and heard in one particular locality how could men regard Him as a universal, spiritual helper? None ever knew so well as He how best to promote men's spiritual welfare. Therefore, as the time for His departure drew near He said to His disciples, "I tell you the truth. It is expedient for you that I go away. For if I should not go away, you would depend, as now, on my physical presence. You could not even understand me. You need to become more and more spiritual. So I am going away. But I shall not leave you alone. The Spirit of God will come and be ever with you. I have done my peculiar work as a concrete human revelation of the Father. Now the universal, invisible Spirit will come and do His work. Primarily He will explain me to you. He will make you understand who I am, and the spiritual meaning of my words and conduct which you cannot now understand. And He will always continue to be with all my brethren and to guide them in all things." Now, since this is Christ's teaching, and since Christianity is loyalty to the living Christ, we may say that the simplicity of Christianity is that it is living by the help of Christ under the guidance of the Spirit of God. That is, the Holy Spirit of God is the spiritual revealer of the Christ who was the concrete revealer of God. Christ said the "Holy Spirit shall take of the things of me and show them to you."

Prior to Jesus Christ men's conceptions of God and of the true relations between God and men were so vague and mistaken that they did not know God as Father. But God so revealed Himself through the life, teachings, sufferings, and resurrection of Jesus that we may say that Jesus is the fullest human expression of God, by which He makes us know Him as the Father of our spirits. But men are still so unspiritual that even with Christ's help they cannot adequately apprehend the Father and walk as His sons without the further and constant help of the Holy Spirit. Owing to men's low, sinful condition they get a wrong conception of God and live without sympathetic obedience to Him. Therefore they need Christ to reveal the Father and help them to live as His sons. Vague and wrong conceptions of God and of their relations to Him are men's first great lack. This Christ supplies. Their next great lack is that even when they get better conceptions, they forget God and live as if He were not. The Holy Spirit, who ever lives with God's sons, supplies this second lack. He makes God a *present* God. He shows that a risen Christ means an ever-living Christ, and that His help does not depend on our visible sight of Him. The Spirit shows Christ's brethren that they have a union with Christ which is ever constant and indissoluble, which in Biblical language is expressed by the term *in* Christ.

Now, how are men to know for themselves whether these things are so or not? In the same vital way as that in which they know anything, *i. e.*, by actual experience. In Biblical language, "As many as are led by the Spirit of God they are the sons of God." "The Spirit beareth witness with our spirit; that we are the children of God." Let a man stop and ask himself, "Is there anyone who has intercourse with my spirit? Is there some voice which speaks to my soul? Is there someone who strengthens the better impulses of my heart? Does he use the example and words and power of Christ or not?" These are simple, natural questions which any man may ask for himself and to which he can, if wise, give answers. Persons who truly take Christ's help can honestly give intelligible answers. Christ definitely said that the Holy Spirit would help the spirits of men and would use Him in this work. There are men who can honestly say that this thing is true in their lives. If true of some, others can test it for themselves. Let a man earnestly desire to know God, see if he will not find the life of Christ most helpful to him. As he brings Christ in any way into connection with his life, see if he does not have inward spiritual impulses. Is it not the most reasonable explanation of those impulses that God by His Spirit is helping the man to walk as His son? This is the explanation offered by Christianity.

In religious matters there are two ways of trying to ascertain truth. One is the purely intellectual method, according to which one asks an argument to the intellect before accepting anything. Thus, for example, according to this method, one would not believe in God till His existence and attributes had been proved. But neither you nor I should much respect even the intellect of a man who would not have anything to do with his mother until he had asked for and examined the intellectual proof of her existence and attributes. Nor should we think that a mother would be of much use to a man who believed in her only because he had asked and received proofs of her existence and character. Similarly, because God *is* the Father of every man and *is* constantly acting as his Father, I do not respect the intellectual condition of men who do not recognize that there is a God until they have been through a process of argument proving His existence. Just as we know men more by association than by argument, so we know God more by association than by argument. Reasoning has its proper place in determining our relations with men, and also in ascertaining what is from God. Christianity has from the first had to give and has gladly given proper and adequate proofs, so far as reason requires them. Nevertheless, the strong thing in Christianity is that it is fitted for the *whole* of man, and its strongest proof is supplying all the needs of men in the simple, vital way of life in all departments. The sound way of trying to ascertain religious truth is the way of making reason and experience go hand in hand. There is such overwhelming historical and experimental evidence for believing that Jesus Christ lived and was substantially as described in the New Testament that the only sensible thing is to act as if that were so, and then to test for yourself whether you need His help by the simple, natural way which I have described, *i. e.*, by personal association with Him. Every thoughtful person knows that personal influence is the greatest influence. When personal association is continuous and spiritual, and includes both the great and little matters of life, it is a transforming power. I have shown that such trustful, intimate, personal association is what Jesus desires and offers to every man. Also I have shown how it is feasible for everyone and for you.

It is feasible, first, by a careful, thoughtful use of the biography of Jesus as written in the four gospels. With this should be used its supplement in the Acts of the Apostles and in the letters of St. Paul and other apostles, because these writings show how association with Jesus Christ affected those early Christians, and how they finally understood Him.

Secondly, Christianity teaches that Christ is now living and in personal relations with us all. If true, this enables us to have personal intercourse with Him in a vital way. It is a thing which every man can test for himself. Paul was the most bitter persecutor of Christians. He became the chief missionary of this faith. He says this change was due to personal intercourse with Christ. If Jesus Christ is even a true religious teacher, this claim is true, because the most important point of His teaching was that He was to be forever with His followers to help them.

Thirdly, the Spirit of God is said by Christ to live with men and to take of Him and to make Him real to men. You and I can test this for ourselves.

The results of trustful, personal association with Christ have always been to lead men to higher and higher views regarding Him, and to make them grow more and more like Him. His earliest disciples from regarding Him as a teacher grew to regard Him more and more as Saviour and Lord. They also grew more and more into His likeness. Paul could honestly say, "I do not live, but Christ lives in me." That was no exaggeration. He was controlled by the mind and spirit of Christ. Whoever lives in trustful, intimate intercourse with Jesus Christ, the Son of God, comes into filial relations with God as Father, and he knows that it is Christ who helps him into this changed life. Now, my friend, will you not try this vital way for yourself? Never mind what anyone else thinks about Christ. Never mind whether things have been put forward which do not seem right to you. Have trustful, intimate personal association with Christ, and you will be helped by Him. You will be helped in your belief. You will be helped in your life. And the more you trust Him and take His help, and follow Him, the more you will grow like Him.

VIII

HOW GANGARAM BECAME ACQUAINTED WITH GOD

PEOPLE in America often wonder how the missionary in India presents Christ to common, plain people there. So I will give you an illustration of the way in which one missionary tries to make God seem vitally great and good and near to every man through the revelation which Christ has made of Him. One of the advantages of being a missionary in India is that with ordinary people religion is there always a natural, proper subject of conversation. It is mainly with people who have come under Western ways and ideas that a Christian has to be careful about quickly introducing a religious topic into conversation. But with the average man one does not need to wait or to beat around the bush before speaking of distinctly Christian things. Suppose that a plain man, who knows nothing of Christianity except that there is now a considerable Christian community in Ahmednagar, and that in a particular house lives a missionary who is a leader of Christians, comes to my house largely out of curiosity. The following would be a way in which I might talk to him. When he knocks on the door, or through a servant sends a message to my room that he wishes to see me, and I say, "Come in," I should first ask, "What is your name?" He might say, "Gangaram," which is as common a name as John or Charles in America. Then I might say, "Do you know my name? It is Hume." Then he would say, "Hume Saheb," *i. e.*, Mr. Hume. Then I would ask, "What is your business?" and he might reply, "I am a carpenter." Then I might say, "Let me tell you my business. It is to help men to become acquainted with God." This makes him look surprised, because he has never heard of such an occupation before. Then I might ask, "Gangaram, are you acquainted with God?" Of course he looks as surprised as if I had asked, "Are you acquainted with the Queen or the Governor?" Then I say, "Gangaram, I am somewhat acquainted with God. It is my business to help men to get acquainted with Him. I will explain it to you so that you can understand. Men get acquainted with God in just the very same way as that in which they get acquainted with men. There is no different way. Just as I have only one pair of outward eyes and outward ears, and have to get all my outward knowledge about everyone through those eyes and ears, so I have only one pair of inward eyes and inward ears, and have to get all my inward knowledge of everyone, of men and of God, through those eyes and ears, by using them in just the same way. What does it mean to be acquainted with anyone? It does not mean to see that man's face, but his mind and heart. There are hundreds of men whose faces we often see, with whom we are not acquainted, because we do not see their minds and hearts. To be acquainted with anyone means to know what he often thinks about, what he is interested in, what he is trying to do, what he is glad for or sorry for, what his hopes and ideals are. Now, there are four ways in which I get acquainted with men, *i. e.*, see what is regularly going on in their minds and hearts; and in the very same ways I get acquainted with

God, *i. e.*, know what is going on in His mind and heart, *i. e.*, I know what He is trying to do, what He is glad for and sorry for, and so I secure intimacy with Him.

"One way in which I get acquainted with men is through letters. Here is a letter from a man who lives ten thousand miles away, whose face I have never seen and may never see. But we write letters to each other. In these letters we say what we are thinking about, and interested in, and what we are trying to do, what we are glad for and sorry for, what our hopes and ideals are; we tell one another how each is getting on; each says what he would like the other to do for him, and inquires what he can do for the other. Through such letters we are becoming truly acquainted, *i. e.*, we see one another's mind and heart, and are drawn to one another. Now, is there anything which men can do which God cannot also do? Men can write letters and get acquainted through them. Do not you suppose that God also can do the same?" Of course, Gangaram looks somewhat surprised, but says that of course God can do whatever men can do. Then I say, "Not only *can* God write letters, but He *has* written many. I have some of His letters in my house now. Here is one, and I will read a part of it to you." Then, of course, I would not open a big book, because that would not seem like a letter. But I usually have in small form a Gospel on my table. Taking up the Gospel of Luke, I say, "Here is a letter from God, in which He has expressed just what my friend expressed in the first letter which I showed you, viz., what He is thinking about, and interested in, and wishing to do; what he is glad for and sorry for; what He wants me to do for Him, and what He wishes to do for me. Therefore by reading this letter I see what is in the mind and heart of God, and so I get acquainted with Him and come to understand and to appreciate Him and am drawn to Him. If you will more and more find out what is in this letter from God and act up to what He wishes in it, you, too, can get acquainted with God. Now I will read something from this letter."

Then I might open at the fifteenth chapter of Luke and say: "In this place in this letter it says that God is like any man, just such a man as you are, just such a man as I am, just like all the men about us. It says that God is like a man who had a hundred sheep. One evening when this shepherd brought his flock home and counted them, he found one missing. What did he say? 'I don't care; let the thing go; I have ninety-nine sheep left'? Of course not. No shepherd ever felt like that. Why not? In the first place, because that sheep was worth money to that shepherd—worth from three to five rupees—and no man is willing to lose money if he can help it. And another reason was because that shepherd had come to feel an interest in that sheep, since he had taken care of it for a long time. So immediately he left the ninety-nine safe sheep in the fold and started to find the lost one. First he went west toward Nepti, but could not find it there. Then he went north toward Savedi, but could not find it there. Then east toward Ferribag, but could not find it. Then he hurried south toward Walki, because it was getting dark; and he asked everyone whom he met if he had seen a stray sheep. And like every Eastern shepherd he often called the name of the sheep. At last he heard a little 'Ba-a' and said, 'I believe that is my sheep.' He called again and went in that direction, and at last he found the poor thing caught in a thicket. It could not get out, its fleece was torn, and it was all in a-tremble because it was dark, and it could hear the wolves howling. What did he do? Did he give the sheep a good kick and say, 'You have made me lots of trouble to-day; I will give you a good beating when I get home'? Not at all. He said, 'You poor, poor thing; I am so sorry for you.' And, like every shepherd, he took it tenderly out of the thicket and lifted it upon his shoulders, two legs on one side and two on the other, and carried it home and spoke kindly to it all the way, and took extra care of it that night. And he was so pleased that he called all his friends together and told them all about it. He did not speak of his troubles, but of his joy in finding the lost sheep. And it says in this letter that that is just what God is like. He is your shepherd, and you are His sheep. But you are worth far more to Him than that sheep was to that shepherd; worth far more than three or five rupees. And He has done far more for you than that shepherd had done for that sheep. But you, too, are lost. For, when you said to me that you are not acquainted with God, that means that you have strayed away from Him. A sheep is lost which does not know the way to its fold. And you are lost in the thicket of ignorance of God. But He is trying to find you, and He will do His best to get you out of it, and to take you home to be with Him where you can be safe. You do not yet know how He feels and talks and deals with men. But He is most eager for you, and He needs you so much that He is trying to find you and all other lost sheep like you, and He has sent me to tell you this.

"Now the letter goes on to say that God is not only like a man, but like a woman; just such a woman as your wife and my wife. This woman had ten pieces of silver. One day when she counted her money one piece was gone. What did she say? Did she say, 'I don't care; I have nine pieces left'? Of course not. You know the proverb that says you can buy ten needles for the smallest copper coin, but that a woman cries if she loses one needle. Then how much worse that woman felt when she had lost a piece of silver. So she did what your or my wife would do. She tried to find the lost coin. But when she could not find it she lighted a lamp, because the room had no windows, and she swept its earthen floor and then threw the dirt which she had gathered up and down in a fan till at last she saw the silver bit. Then she was so pleased that she called her women friends together and told them all about it, and said, 'Rejoice with me, for I have found the money that was lost.' And the letter says that is how God feels. Gangaram, you are God's money. He needs you. You are worth much more to Him than that coin was to that woman. The place for money is not in the dirt, where it is worth nothing, but to be clean and in its owner's hand, so that he can do with it what he wants. You are in the dirt of ignorance and carelessness; that is, you are lost, and not in God's hand, where He can use you to do some good work. But He is trying to find and to clean you so that He can do some good work by you. He is so anxious for you that He sent me here to tell you this.

"Then the letter goes on to say that God is like a rich man who had two boys. The younger boy had got into bad company, and was not contented and made much trouble. He kept nagging his father and saying, 'Father, there is no fun here in this little village; no chance to make much money, or to get a reputation. I want to go to Bombay. That is a big place, where there is lots of fun and chances to make money. Let me have some money and go there. Some day you will see me come back with a big bag of money.' But the father replied, 'My boy, I have lived longer than you. It is easier to lose money than to make it. Those companions of yours are not good. They are sure to get you into trouble.' But the boy kept nagging his father, and at last he got his money and went off. He thought he was going to have a grand time. He had fun for a while. But his companions fleeced him. He lost all his money, and pawned his clothes and fell sick. And plague and famine all around made him think he would die. Then he said, 'I am a fool. Here I am dying with hunger, and even the servants at home have plenty of everything.

I will go home.' So he started. But when he came near to the house he thought how his older brother and the servants might laugh, and say, 'A big bag of money he has brought.' So he felt ashamed and stopped a moment behind a tree. But, Gangaram, what had been happening in that house all those days? Every day the mother had cried. Every single day that father's heart had been heavy. If he knew of anyone's going to Bombay he would say, 'If you see my boy, tell him his mother is dying for lack of him, and tell him to come home.' And at the moment that the boy stood hesitating under the tree the father was thinking, 'Where is my boy now?' And as he looked out he said, 'Who is that? It looks like my boy,' and down the road he ran and they both threw their arms around one another and both cried. The boy said, 'Father, I have been a naughty boy. I have made you and mother sorry. I have wasted your money. I do not ask you to take me into the family again. But please try me as a servant.' Then the father said, 'My boy, my boy! Don't you say another word. Your mother will be a new woman to-day. Come right into the house.' And he pulled him in and left him with his mother in an inner room, where both could cry and be glad, while he went and told the servants, 'Make a great dinner to-day. This is the happiest day this house has ever known. This son of ours who was as good as dead is alive again and at home.' Now, Gangaram, that is just what God is like. He is your father. You are His boy. You have been foolish and done a great many wrong things. These have caused you much trouble. But your God, too, has suffered because you have lived away from Him. But He longs for you and needs you, and He wants you to come and live with Him. He cannot bear to have any son of His suffer in ignorance and sin. He wants everyone to live near Him as a loyal son. And He wants you and me to know this, and therefore has sent us this letter.

"Now, Gangaram, I could tell you a great deal more that there is in this letter. But there is a second way in which we get acquainted with men and with God. Through messengers, also, we get acquainted with men. That is, we find out what is in their minds and hearts, what they are thinking about, and trying to do; what they are glad for and sorry for; what they wish to do for us, and what they wish us to do for them. Yonder in that house lives the Collector, who is my friend. Often he sends a messenger to me to say what he wants me to know. He sometimes sends me a paper or a book, and asks me for an American magazine or book. He asks me to come to see him at a certain time and place. He wants to know about various things in which we both are interested. And in this way we become better acquainted. Now men get acquainted with God also in the very same way. He sends messengers to men to tell them what is in His mind and heart: what He is trying to do; what He is glad for and sorry for; what He wishes us to do for Him and what He wishes to do for us. And that is just what I am—God's messenger to you. There are things which He is very anxious that you should know and do, and so He has sent me to you. Now listen.

"More than nineteen hundred years ago a very wonderful thing happened to the northwest of Kanhur over there, some twenty-five hundred miles away. It was so wonderful that now almost everyone counts time from that event. Every letter that is stamped in the post-office is stamped with that date. Every newspaper that is published in this country dates from that event, though it happened in a distant land years ago. It was like this: Your own religion says that the god Vishnu took ten incarnations. The first was a fish, the second was a tortoise, the third was a boar, and so on. Personally I do not believe this, because it does not seem sensible, and I do not think God would do what was not sensible. I would not become a fish or a tortoise or a boar, if I wanted to help you. You could not understand fish language or fish experiences. However, I do not care very much whether you believe it or not. But there is one thing which is at the heart of all those stories about Vishnu's incarnations which I do believe with all my heart; it is that when man is in trouble you may be sure that God will try to help him. And that is what happened nineteen hundred years ago. When men could not understand what was in the mind and heart of God, He said, 'I will go to help them.' But He came in a sensible and helpful way; that is, He came as a man. Everyone can understand human experiences. A tear and a smile mean and express the very same thing in every part of the world, even though men may not understand one another's words. So because men did not understand properly what was in God's heart and mind, He took an incarnation in a very great and good man to help men truly to understand what God is like; how He thinks and feels; what He is glad for and sorry for; what He wishes to do for us, and us to do for Him. Now the name of this incarnation was Jesus, which means Helper; and He also was sometimes called Christ, which means the appointed one, *i. e.*, He was the Helper whom God appointed to come and reveal Him. It is from Him that the Christian religion gets its name. And the essence of the Christian religion is that God is like Jesus Christ. Now let me tell you about Him. He was born a baby, and grew up like you and me. He never had any advantages in schools. But He was most intimate with God, whom He always recognized as with Him and whom He pleased and whom He sought to reveal to men. His business, like yours, was that of a carpenter. Whenever He made a plow or a door or a window, He made just as good a job as He could. He was most kind to all men and most strong. He gave eyes to the blind, ears to the deaf, and limbs to the lame. He even gave life to the dead. But He did more wonderful things than that. He made the bad good. He made hard-hearted Marwadis [money-lenders], who love money more than anything else, generous and humble. Once when I was in the village of Ambli-Vadgaon a Marwadi came to say that the Mission teacher, Nanaji, who had just been transferred from that village, still owed him four rupees, and he wished me to collect and pay him this sum. I told him that I would speak to Nanaji about it, and, if it was all right, I would see that the small debt was repaid. Just then a poor, paralyzed woman came up to ask for help. She was in rags. So I said to the Marwadi, 'I tell you what I will do. I will take the responsibility of collecting and paying those four rupees now, if you will use part of it in helping to buy a garment for this poor woman. I will pay half the price, and you pay half.' But the Marwadi replied, 'Sir, not one particle will I give.' What do you think of that, Gangaram? Just like a great many Marwadis, wasn't he? There was a poor, paralyzed, half-starved woman of his own town for whom he was not willing to do one thing. Would it be more wonderful to give eyes to the blind, or to give inward eyes to such a money-lender and to make him humble and generous? Well, that is what Jesus Christ did. One day, when He was going through a town called Jericho, a money-lender, like the Ambli-Vadgaon Marwadi, named Zaccheus, a short man, got up into a tree to see Jesus plainly as He was passing along with a great crowd. When Jesus reached the tree, He looked up and said, 'Zaccheus, come down. I would like to go home with you to-day!' The man was amazed and so was the crowd, because everyone knew that he was a hard-hearted, dishonest man who had no religion at all. But the object of Jesus was to make that bad man good, though He did not say so. I would give a great deal to know what Jesus Christ said to Zaccheus in his house. I am pretty sure He did not say anything to him at first about his being bad. I think He may have said, 'Zaccheus, what a nice house you have; how much good you can do to your neighbors and to poor people if you are hospitable and share your house with them. How much good you can do with your money if you are thoughtful and generous with it. You ought to remember that your money and your house are really God's, not your own, and that the only real value of money is that you do good with it in the way in which God wishes you to use His money. Though you may not have thought of this before, I hope you will hereafter.' I am sure He spoke of God as Father of all men, and all men as brothers, and of the blessedness of being good, and of the joy which one can give to Him by being sorry for sin and of living right for the rest of one's life, etc. And, Gangaram, before Jesus Christ left that house, that hard-fisted, hard-hearted money-lender became a changed man. He said with trembling in his voice, 'Sir, I am not the same man I was when I came in with you. You have helped me to see that I am not good. I have never sought anything but money for its own sake. And I have never stopped to consider whether I did right or wrong in getting money. Everyone considers me hard-hearted. I do not suppose one person loves me. But I have made up my mind to become a different man. I will do my best to think up all the men from whom I have squeezed money wrongfully. And I will give four rupees for every rupee which I have taken wrongfully, so far as possible. But I never can find half the people whom I have wronged. So I shall give half of the rest of my property to the poor, and I will try never again to take money wrongfully!' What do you think of that, Gangaram? Did you ever know of any *guru* [spiritual leader] who could do, or did, things like that? But that was what Jesus often did, and now wants to do. He made very bad women penitent and pure and humble. But, strange to say, some of the priests hated Jesus because He taught about God as He did, and they plotted against Him and at last managed to kill Him. But you would not expect that death could defeat such as He, would you? Not at all. They could put Him to death. But they could not keep Him dead, and three days after they had killed Him He rose from the dead, and is alive now and forever will be, and is near everyone to help him. And this letter from which I read to you is principally taken up with telling about Him. That is how it came to be written.

"But there is a third way of getting acquainted with men. It is to talk to them and to hear what they say. That is the way in which you and I are getting acquainted now. You are now finding out what kind of a man I am, what I think about and try to do, what I want to do for you and other men. And I am beginning to know you. Well, is there anything which men do to one another which they cannot do to God and God to them? We can talk to one another. Can we not talk to God? Of course we can. He that made the ear, shall He not hear? Talking to God is what Christians call prayer." Gangaram evidently does not see this plainly. So I say, "I know what troubles you. You cannot see God, and have an idea that if any vow is to be made to Him you need to go to an idol and by it be reminded that He can be told something. But idols are not necessary. They are even a hindrance. Cannot blind people who see nothing outwardly talk to one another just as well as those who have eyes? Wait a minute." Then I step behind a door, and ask, "Can you hear me?" He says, "Yes." Then I say, "Speak to me. Say, 'I hear you.'" He says, "I hear you." Then I return and say, "When we could not see each other we could hear each other just as well as now, when we see one another, because we were near. How near is God to us now? Nearer than we are to each other. He is always right by our side. What does your proverb say, 'Not a leaf stirs without God's moving it.' So God can hear us, hear even our thoughts, and He wishes us to talk to Him. Is there not something which you would like to say to God now?" Then again Gangaram looks confused and says, "What should I say?" I reply, "I will tell you what I think it would be well for you to say to Him. Would it not be well to say, 'I do not know Thee; but I should like to?'" "Yes." "And to say, 'Please make me a better man?'" "Yes." "And 'help me in my business?'" "Yes." "And 'bless my family?'" "Yes." "Well, now, say those four things to God; to the God who is nearer you than I am, right by your side, who is like that shepherd and that woman and that father, and like Jesus Christ. Do not say them to me or to the air, but to God." Again Gangaram looks surprised and perplexed. He does not know how to pray. So I say, "I will help you. Sentence by sentence I will suggest to you what to say, and then you say them to Him; not to the air, and not to me; but to Him." I would not ask Gangaram to close his eyes, because that is no necessary part of prayer, and because he would feel uncomfortable to do so before a stranger. He might imagine that I might make some passes over him with my hands, or work some hocus-pocus. So I take hold of one wrist and hold up his hand to help him feel that he is really himself speaking to someone, and not merely repeating words after me into the air. "Now, Gangaram, say to God what I have suggested to you, and what you really wish to say to Him. Say it to Him, not to me, and not to the air. I am only helping you. But it must be you yourself who is speaking to God, who is right here and who is eager to have you speak to Him. Say, 'O God, I do not know Thee.'" "O God, I do not know Thee." "But I should like to." "But I should like to." "Please make me a better man." "Please make me a better man." "And bless my family." "And bless my family." "Now, Gangaram, God not only *heard* what you said to Him; He *cares*. You have a Hindustani couplet which says:

> "'Do hathawale jitne hain
> Un sabse chod hath,
> Mang usse jiske hain,
> Ab sau karor hath.'

[Withhold your hand from one that has only two hands (*i. e.*, men), ask of Him who has a thousand million hands.] If He has a thousand million hands, how many hearts has He? A thousand million, and He cares for you, and is ready to answer your wish.

"But do you suppose He can talk as well as hear? Of course He can. He that made the tongue, shall He not speak? He talks straight to every single person every day; only He talks in His own way. Many people do not know that He is talking because they do not understand how He talks. I will tell you. Animals make a loud noise when they talk. The donkey brays, the dog barks, the cow lows. But cultivated people, when they talk, speak low. But God talks lower and stiller than the most cultivated man or woman. He talks something as my wife sometimes talks to our children and to me. Every morning when it is time to rise she opens the windows and lets the light into the room, and in that way she says to the children, 'Now get up.' And every night when she puts them to bed, she puts out the light, and that is her way of saying, 'Now, go to sleep.' That is just the way in which God speaks to everyone in the world every day. Every morning *He* opens the windows and lets in the light, and in this way *says*, 'Get up, everyone.' Every night *He* puts out the light, and so in His way *says*, 'Go to sleep, everyone.' Every time that He sends rain, He says in His own way, 'Look out, get the fields ready to sow,' etc. Every time that He sends a customer to you He says to you, 'Now is your chance to earn money. But be sure to make a good job!' That is,

God speaks to everyone by what He *does*, just as men do. The only trouble is that people do not feel well enough acquainted with Him to know that this *is* one of His ways of talking. But it really is. God talks by everything that He does.

"And another of His quiet ways of talking is by putting thoughts into men's minds. That is one way in which your wife and my wife talk to us. Without saying one word out loud, by her looks my wife often tells me what she wishes to say. And the more I get acquainted with her, the more I know what she is thinking about, and what she wishes, and what she is glad for or sorry for, by the thoughts which she puts into my mind, without speaking loud. So God talks to us by putting thoughts into our minds. Every good thought which ever comes into your or my mind, Gangaram, is God talking to us. It does not happen. It is His voice. But how little we realize that that is God's principal way of communicating with His children! I will tell you what I think God may be saying to you now. I think He may be putting into your mind this thought, 'These are the most wonderful and the best things which I ever heard.'" "That is so, Saheb." "Well, Gangaram, that is God speaking to you." "You would do well to act as if these things are true." "Yes." "Well, that, too, is God's voice. And every good thought that ever will come into your mind will be God's voice to you.

"Now, Gangaram, the fourth way in which to get acquainted with men is to live with them, to go about with them, to see them do their work, and to take their help in your work. And that is also the way to get acquainted with God. It is good to read His letter, to hear what His messengers say, to talk to Him, and to hear Him talk; but all these are not enough if you do not live with Him and have Him live inside of you as He wants to live. Looking at bread does not feed anyone. The bread must be inside him. Hearing about water does not satisfy anyone's thirst. It must be inside of him. So hearing *about* God will not make you acquainted with Him. He must be *in* your mind and heart. If what I have said goes into one ear and out of the other, that will not make you acquainted with God. You must keep these things and Him in your heart and mind. Live as though they were true. Tell your wife and children and neighbors about them. Recognize every customer as from God, and make every plow and door and window as if you were making it for God. Recognize every good thought as from Him. Often look up and speak to Him. In these ways, Gangaram, you can become truly acquainted with God. He knows all about you, and He wants you to become acquainted with Him.

"Now, good-bye, Gangaram. Come and see me as often as you can. When you can, come to our church over there. You may not know what its bell says. It was made in America, but when it says, 'Ding, dong,' that means, 'Come, come.' Whenever it says, 'Ding, dong, ding, dong,' it means, 'Come, come, everyone; come, come, Gangaram; come, come.' Come whenever you can. Whenever you come there you will hear more from this letter of God's; His messenger will tell you His messages; we shall talk to Him, and He will talk back to us, by putting good thoughts into our hearts; and then we will act as if we were living with Him."

Friends in America, is there any other way to become acquainted with God here than the way of the old, old story as Gangaram heard it? Our Lord Jesus Christ truly said, "This is life eternal; not that we should go by and by to a safe place called heaven, but that we should become acquainted with God here and now, through Jesus Christ, whom He has sent." *This* is life eternal, to be intimate with God; to think His thoughts with Him; to respond to His love for us; to share His love for our brother-men and sister-women; to be filial to Him in our plans and lives, by the desire to please Him and to have His blessed will done everywhere as it is done in heaven. This is what Jesus Christ helps men to do as no one else, and why we need to take His help and become Christians. *This* is life eternal, to be acquainted with God. And the better that we ourselves become acquainted with Him the more we shall gladly do all we can to enable Him to win every single human child of His in every land to become acquainted with Him and to live with Him as a son.

INDEX